P9-AZU-613

THE GRAND CENTRAL OYSTER BAR & RESTAURANT COMPLETE SEAFOOD COOKBOOK

THE GRAND CENTRAL OYSTER BAR & RESTAURANT COMPLETE SEAFOOD COOKBOOK

Compiled and Revised by
chef Sandy Ingber

STEWART, TABORI & CHANG
NEW YORK

First hard cover edition , 1997
First revised paperback edition, 1999

Published in North America by

Oyster Bar Press
New York, New York

Distributed in the United States by
Stewart, Tabori and Chang,
a division of U.S. Media Holdings, Inc.
575 Broadway, New York, NY 10012

Distributed in Canada by
General Publishing Company Ltd.
30 Lesmill Road, Don Mills
Ontario, Canada, M3B 2T6

Copyright © 1996, 1997,1999 by the United Brody Corporation
Packaged and edited by Freundlich Communications, Inc.
Cookbook Design by Jennifer Woodward
Principle Photography by Richard Martinot
Photograph on p. iii by Eugene Vos

Origination: Regent Publishing Services, Ltd., Hong Kong
Printed in China

Library of Congress Catalog Card number: 96-69813

10 9 8 7 6 5 4 3 2 1

THE
GRAND CENTRAL
OYSTER BAR & RESTAURANT
COMPLETE SEAFOOD
COOKBOOK

PREFACE

In 1977, three years after Jerome Brody had reopened, re-invented, and revitalized the old Grand Central Oyster Bar, and set it on its path towards becoming America's premier seafood restaurant, The Oyster Bar published a relatively slim volume of recipes that elicited so much praise for its classic simplicity and reliability, that when it finally went out of print, we hatched the plan to publish another, more ambitious Oyster Bar cookbook. It would be a grand gathering from the huge selection of offerings that have been featured at The Oyster Bar over its long history, emphasizing the recipes and techniques we have developed in the last 25 years.

As we delved back into the records and recollections of the several distinguished chefs who have served at The Oyster Bar, we not only reacquainted ourselves with some neglected classics, but were forced to evolve and refine the techniques and recipes that characterize today's Oyster Bar & Seafood Restaurant.

Having this large and historic bulk of material before me struck home to me what is undoubtedly the largest single change in our seafood cuisine. Where once our fish and shellfish came only from American waters—and of those, mostly from Maine to the Chesapeake—now our menu is international. Even our trademark, the oyster, can be served 12 months a year, and not only with months containing the letter "R," because refrigerated jet transportation has made it possible for us to serve the harvest of the Southern Hemisphere, such as oysters from Chile and New Zealand, and to serve fresh everyday such delicacies as Dover Sole from the English Channel and salmon from Norway. With new varieties came new recipes.

This new edition of the cookbook arrives just as the beautifully restored Grand Central Station draws hundreds of thousands of new admirers, many of whom are discovering The Oyster Bar for the first time. Even more than when the Bard first penned his prophetic lines, is it nowadays true that "All the world's your oyster."

Michael Garvey
Vice-president & general manager

WELCOME TO THE GRAND CENTRAL OYSTER BAR & RESTAURANT

The Oyster Bar first opened its doors in 1913 on the lower level of Grand Central Terminal. Woodrow Wilson was President, the United States was on the threshold of World War I, and Prohibition was just six years away. New York City was slowly emerging as a literary and artistic center, and little "salons" that attracted writers and artists and dilettantes were starting to spring up in Greenwich Village and in other parts of the city. The resplendent new Grand Central Terminal opened its doors that year too, on the site of what formerly had been the old and rundown train depot. People flocked to see the new terminal that was then as now considered an engineering marvel.

For almost 60 years the old Oyster Bar remained a landmark. But if the truth be known, the long-lived acceptance of the restaurant was based more on its being located at the hub of America's long-haul passenger train system than on excellence. With the decline of the long-haul passenger train system, came the decline of the restaurant. It had no position among New York restaurants, and while thousands of commuters passed by everyday, very few went inside to eat.

In 1974, when I was approached by the New York Metropolitan Transit Authority to take it over, the old restaurant had been bankrupt and empty for two years, having become in its last days not much more than a sad, old coffee shop. Reluctantly, I inspected what remained of its former grandness. The elegant marble columns you see in the restaurant today were then painted aquamarine over wallpaper. The wall covering was yellow Cello-tex™. The furniture was upholstered yellow, in unsettling contrast with the red table cloths.

Despite the obvious drawbacks and failures of the old restaurant, I thought that if we could develop a strong merchandising concept, the 440 seat capacity had real potential. But it would be up to us to invent a new restaurant—from menu to decor—which would make us a destination restaurant.

Today's customer of the Grand Central Oyster Bar and Restaurant can hardly imagine that the old Oyster Bar, while its title suggested seafood, was not, in fact, a seafood restaurant. Its oyster stew had become famous, but the rest of the menu could best be described as "continental." Our job of invention would start from scratch—but seafood it would be.

To prepare for the decision, my wife and I toured the best-known seafood restaurants in Manhattan, Brooklyn, New Jersey, and the rest of the metropolitan area, and they were invariably full—even when the cuisine was ordinary. That is what decided me to take a chance—the same kind of chance I had taken with restaurants such as the Forum of The Twelve Caesars, the Rainbow Room, the Four Seasons, and Gallagher's. And so, in 1974, I entered into a lease with the MTA, and embarked on inventing the Grand Central Oyster Bar & Restaurant.

The *sine qua non* of our hoped-for success was that we would need a network of the best suppliers, and my wife, Marlene and I personally sought it out. In Maine we searched for lobster. In Gloucester, Massachusetts, for the best fish from the Grand Banks; in Virginia, for oysters and crabs from Chesapeake Bay. To this day, the Grand Central Oyster Bar & Restaurant continues to cultivate and reach out to a great number of international suppliers, ranging from large corporations to individual fishermen, with whom over the years we have developed a privileged relationship.

Confident that we had ample access to the best, fresh seafood, our next step was to test our menu in our own kitchens. And so we spent a tremendous amount of time deciding not only what to have on the menu but on methods of preparation. Even an apparently basic technique like broiling was subject to the closest scrutiny. But whatever we prepared, we wanted our hallmark to be the best, fresh fish available, presented in a bright, clean, manner.

Because we aspired to be a great American seafood restaurant, we set out to develop a superb American white wine list. As carefully as we had sought out our seafood suppliers, that is how exhaustively we selected our wine wholesalers and vintners, who, to this day, have named the white wine cellars of the Grand Central Oyster Bar among the best in the country. We won The Brotherhood of the Knights of the Vine "Gold Vine Award" in 1978 and 1979. We began serving wine by the glass in 1993, offering choices from among 70 different wines. "The Wine Spectator" honored us with its Award of Excellence in 1996. And, yes, we do serve excellent red wines also.

Our success did not happen over night. But over the years we have more than quadrupled our business, which is proof that we have been pleasing our guests and benefiting from the best kind of support any restaurant can ever get: word-of-mouth. In this marketplace a restaurant opens and gets a lot of play, but what happens a year later? What happens 20 years later? To have flourished for these 20 years, that is success.

Still we are testing, still looking for unusual sources, not just for lobsters, but in this age of refrigerated air transport, we look towards the Southern Hemisphere for benefits such as summer oysters. We search out products from the ever-increasing stocks made available through aqua-culture. We testcook new sauces to accommodate today's trend towards less butter and cream. Every day we monitor the computer records of what is popular with our customers and what is not, so that our whole menu, which is new each day, stays in tune with our guests' preferences.

Old and new friends come back regularly—some of them every day—for some of the 16 or 17 varieties of oysters we carry fresh daily or a favorite dish that they insist doesn't taste the same anywhere else. The Oyster Bar & Restaurant with its high, vaulted ceiling and the architectural grandness of an age gone by has an ambiance now that makes it different from any other restaurant in the world, and since people enjoy our cuisine, they come back again and again.

Jerome Brody

TABLE OF

CONTENTS

THE GRAND CENTRAL

OYSTER ®

BAR & RESTAURANT

SAUCES

SAUCE AMANDINE

Ingredients

8 Tbsp (1 stick) sweet
 butter
2 oz blanched almonds,
 sliced
2 tsp fresh lemon juice
1Tbsp chopped parsley

ABOUT 1 cup

Melt butter in a small skillet over low heat.

Add almonds and sauté until golden brown.

Stir in lemon juice.

Add parsley.

SAUCE LOBSTER AMÉRICAINE

ABOUT 1 1/2 CUPS

In a small skillet sauté vegetables in oil until translucent.

Add tomatoes and purée, tarragon, and lobster bodies.

Stir in 1 cup white wine and 4 cups water, and simmer for about 60 minutes.

Strain broth and reserve.

Grind shells in blender, adding a little broth as necessary.

Put shells back into the broth, and stir and strain into a stock pot.

Bring to a boil, and add heavy cream, salt, pepper, and flamed brandy.

Thicken with roux and cook for 1 minutes.

Strain and recheck for proper seasoning.

Ingredients

2 carrots, diced
4 ribs celery, diced
2 shallots (or scallions), diced
1 Tbsp corn oil
1/4 cup tomato purée
1 cup fresh tomatoes, peeled, cooked, and finely chopped
4 garlic cloves
1 Tbsp fresh parsley, finely chopped
1 Tbsp fresh tarragon, roughly, chopped
3 Tbsp brandy. flamed off
1 tsp black pepper corns
4 bay leaves
5 lb lobster bodies, uncooked
1 cup heavy cream
1/4 tsp cayenne pepper
salt and white pepper to taste

ANCHOVY BUTTER

Ingredients

4 Tbsp (1/2 stick) sweet
     butter
4 anchovy fillets, finely
     chopped
1/2 tsp fresh parsley,
     minced
few drops fresh lemon
     juice to taste
1 Tbsp shallots, minced
2 Tbsp white wine
1/2 tsp garlic, minced

ABOUT 1/4 CUP

Soften butter in a small bowl.

Stir in anchovy fillets, parsley, fresh lemon juice
to taste, garlic, shallots, and white wine.

Melt over broiled oyster or broiled fish.

BÉCHAMEL

MAKES 2 CUPS

In a sauce pan, melt butter over low heat.

Blend in flour a little at a time, stirring with a wire whisk, until a ball of flour can be gathered from the bits of butter and flour (this is called the *roux*).

Raise flame to medium-high, and pour in all the liquid, onion, bay, and cloves.

When the liquid comes to a boil, continue whisking until sauce is smooth.

Cook 15 minutes and strain.

Remove from heat and add salt, condiments, pepper, etc., as called for by the variations in individual recipes using béchamel as a basis.

Ingredients

2 tsp sweet butter
3 tsp flour
1 small onion
2 bay leaves
2 cloves
white pepper to taste
2 cups milk
salt to taste

BÉARNAISE SAUCE

Ingredients

1/2 tsp whole
 peppercorns
1/4 cup tarragon wine
 vinegar
1/4 cup dry white wine
1 Tbsp shallots (or
 scallions), finely
 chopped
3 Tbsp fresh tarragon,
 minced (or 2 tsp dried
 tarragon)
1 Tbsp fresh parsley, finely
 chopped
1 1/2 cups basic
 Hollandaise sauce (see
 p.20)
salt to taste
dash of freshly ground
 white pepper

ABOUT 1 1/2 CUPS

In a small heavy saucepan bring tarragon vinegar, wine, shallots/scallions, and 1 Tbsp or 1 tsp (dried) of the tarragon to a brisk boil.

Boil until liquid is reduced to about 1 or 2 oz.

Strain liquid through a fine sieve into a small bowl, pressing down hard on the shallots/scallions and herbs with a wooden spoon before discarding them.

Whisk liquid, 2 Tbsp or 1 tsp (dried) tarragon, and parsley into the Hollandaise sauce.

Add salt and freshly ground white pepper to taste.

Keep warm, but not hot.

BEURRE BLANC

ABOUT 2 CUPS

In a small saucepan combine the shallots, white wine vinegar, and white wine.

Reduce on medium flame until almost all the fluid is gone.

Add heavy cream and reduce again by two thirds.

Put the reduction into the top part of a double boiler and incorporate the butter by whisking it gradually into the reduction. Pass the sauce through a fine sieve.

Keep warm, but not hot.

NOTE
To prepare red wine *beurre blanc* substitute red wine vinegar and red wine for their white counterparts.

1/4 cup white wine vinegar (see note)
1/4 cup white wine (see note)
1 cup chopped shallots
1/2 cup heavy cream
1 cup sweet butter at room temperature

CHAMPAGNE SAUCE

Ingredients

3 Tbsp clarified butter
3 Tbsp flour
1 cup heavy cream
1 cup Champagne
1 cup fish stock
salt and pepper to taste
2 shallots, diced
2 bay leaves
1/4 tsp black peppercorns

ABOUT 2 CUPS

Reduce Champagne and fish stock, shallots, bay leaves, peppercorns by half.

Into an enamel or stainless steel saucepan, slowly stir butter, flour.

Cook over medium heat, stirring with a wire whisk or wooden spoon until thickened and smooth.

Cool for 15 minutes.

Strain.

Salt and pepper to taste.

COCKTAIL SAUCE

ABOUT 1 1/2 CUPS

Combine all ingredients and mix well.

Refrigerate in a tightly covered container until ready to serve.

Ingredients

3/4 cup ketchup
3/4 cup chili sauce
prepared horseradish
    to taste
1 tsp Worcestershire sauce
juice of 1 small lemon
4 dashes of Tabasco sauce
1 garlic clove, minced or
    mashed
salt to taste
freshly ground black
    pepper to taste

HORSERADISH SAUCE

Ingredients

1/4 cup prepared
  horseradish, drained
  and squeezed
1 pt sour cream
1 tsp salt
dash of freshly ground
  white pepper
1 small onion, minced
1 tsp white vinegar
2 Tbsp fresh dill, finely
  chopped

ABOUT 2 CUPS

Thoroughly mix horseradish, sour cream, salt, pepper, onion, vinegar, and dill in a bowl.

DIJON MUSTARD SAUCE

Ingredients

2 tsp onion, minced
1 Tbsp Dijon mustard
1 1/2 tsp sugar
2 Tbsp corn or peanut oil
2 Tbsp white vinegar
1 Tbsp heavy cream
2 hard-cooked egg yolks,
  minced

ABOUT 1 CUP

Combine all ingredients and mix thoroughly.

EGG SAUCE

ABOUT 1 CUP

Melt butter in the top part of a double boiler.

Stir in flour and salt with a wooden spoon and keep mixture warm over hot but not boiling water.

Slowly blend in cream/half-and-half and continue stirring until sauce is creamy and smooth.

Add chopped eggs and parsley.

The sauce may be sprinkled with a few drops of fresh lemon juice, tabsco and Worchestershire) when serving.

Ingredients

2 Tbsp (1/4 stick) sweet
  butter
2 Tbsp flour
1/2 tsp salt
1 cup light cream, or
  half-and-half
2 hard-cooked eggs, finely
  chopped
1 tsp fresh parsley, minced
lemon juice (optional)
2 drops Tabasco
2 drops Worchestershire

FISH VELOUTÉ
(Fish-Flavored White Cream Sauce)

Ingredients

4 Tbsp clarified butter
4 Tbsp flour
1 cup heavy cream
 1/2 cups dry white wine
1/2 cup fish stock

ABOUT 3 CUPS

Heat butter in a large heavy skillet. Over low heat, slowly stir in flour.

With a wire whisk, add heavy cream and whisk until mixture is creamy and smooth.

Add white wine and fish stock.

Continue to whisk until bubbling.

Remove from heat and strain through a fine mesh.

GARLIC-VINEGAR SAUCE

SERVES 4

In a mixing bowl combine all ingredients and allow to stand for at least 1 hour.

Garlic-vinegar sauce is a simple and appropriate dipping sauce for boiled shrimps, clams and oysters.

Ingredients

4 cloves pressed garlic
3/4 cup white vinegar
1/4 cup water
1/4 tsp freshly ground
    black pepper
1/4 tsp salt

SAUCE VERT
(Green Sauce)

Ingredients

1 cup basic mayonnaise
   recipe (see p. 23)
1/4 cup whipped cream
   (see note)
1/4 cup sour cream or
   crême fraiche
1 tsp capers
1 tsp dill pickle, finely
   chopped and drained
2 tsp fresh watercress or
   spinach, minced,
   squeezed, and juice
   saved
1 tsp fresh parsley,
   minced, squeezed and
   juice saved
1/8 tsp horseradish

NOTE
Sour cream may be
eliminated if you prefer
to use 1/2 cup whipped
cream

ABOUT 1 1/2 CUPS

Combine all ingredients well and chill at least 1 hour
before serving.

SAUCE GRIBICHE

ABOUT 1 1/2 CUPS

Combine all ingredients thoroughly and chill for 1 hour before serving.

Ingredients

1 1/4 cups basic
    mayonnaise (see p.23)
1 tsp Dijon mustard
1 tsp capers, finely
    chopped
1 tsp fresh parsley, finely
    chopped
1 tsp dill pickle, finely
    chopped
1 hard-cooked egg, finely
    chopped
salt to taste
freshly ground black
    pepper to taste

CORIANDER AND JALAPEÑO CREAM SAUCE

Ingredients

2 jalepeños, finely
 chopped
2 oz coriander, chopped
8 oz *béchamel*
 (see p. 5)
2 oz heavy cream

ABOUT 1 CUP

Combine all ingredients and mix thoroughly.

Serve immediately so color will hold.

HOLLANDAISE SAUCE
(Blender)

MAKES 3/4 CUP

Place egg yolks, lemon juice, salt, and pepper in the blender and blend for about 2 minutes.

Uncover blender and slowly drizzle in the melted butter while blending.

Stir once with a wooden spoon before serving.

Ingredients

3 egg yolks at room
    temperature
2 Tbsp fresh lemon juice
1/4 tsp salt
dash of freshly ground
    white pepper
8 Tbsp (1 stick) melted
    sweet butter, hot
2 dashes Tabasco

HOLLANDAISE SAUCE (Basic)

Ingredients

3 egg yolks
8 Tbsp sweet butter
1 Tbsp fresh lemon juice
1 Tbsp dry white wine
1/4 tsp salt
2 dashes Tobasco

MAKES 1 CUP

Remove eggs from refrigerator and let stand for about 2 hours until they're at room temperature.

Separate, and set whites aside for another use.

Melt butter, set aside.

In the top part of a double boiler, away from the heat, whisk egg yolks with the white wine briskly, until they begin to get thick and creamy.

VERY SLOWLY blend in the melted butter.

Add the lemon juice and Tobasco.

Add salt.

Keep mixture warm and creamy near a warm oven until ready to serve.

NOTE
Don't let the top bowl of the double boiler touch the water below after the sauce is done.

SAUCE MALTAISE

Ingredients

1 cup freshly squeezed
   blood orange juice,
2 shallots
1 tsp whole black
   peppercorns
1/2 cup white wine
1/2 cup basic Hollandise
   (see p.20)

ABOUT 1 1/2 CUPS

Combine orange juice, shallots, peppercorns, and wine and reduce over medium heat to 1/4 cup.

Strain and let cool slightly.

Add to Basic Hollandaise. Salt and pepper to taste.

MAYONNAISE
(Basic)

ABOUT 1 1/2 CUPS

Whisk egg yolks briskly in a bowl until they begin to get thick and creamy.

Add vinegar, salt, and mustard and whisk for about a minute until well blended.

Slowly add the oil a drop at a time (if oil is added too quickly the mayonnaise will curdle), whisking thoroughly and constantly until about 1/3 cup of the oil has been used.

Add the remaining oil slowly, making sure that it's being absorbed by the eggs and smoothly blended.

NOTE
If mayonnaise separates while being stored in the refrigerator, you can bring it back by slowly beating an egg yolk into the mixture a few drops at a time.

Ingredients
2 egg yolks at room
   temperature
1 Tbsp wine vinegar
1/2 tsp salt
1/2 tsp Dijon mustard
2 cups olive or peanut oil
   (or half and half of
   each)

LOBSTER BUTTER

Ingredients

Shell and body of 1 1 1/2
    lb lobster
5 Tbsp sweet butter
water to cover
bouquet garni (see p. 11)

ABOUT 2 CUPS

Pound the shell pieces in a mortar until they are thoroughly crushed.

Place the pieces of shell and body in a saucepan with the butter.

Add water to cover and the *bouquet garni*. Boil over medium heat for 1/2 hour.

Strain through several thicknesses of cheesecloth into a bowl and chill until butter has formed on the surface of the liquid. Pour off the liquid, and allow the butter to soften at room temperature before using.

MEUNIÉRE
(Lemon Butter)

ABOUT 1/2 CUP

Melt 1 stick butter in a small saucepan over low heat.

Heat clarified butter slowly over low heat until golden brown. Stir in lemon juice and parsley.

Ingredients

8 Tbsp (1 stick) browned
   butter
juice of 2 fresh lemons to
   taste
1 Tbsp fresh parsley, finely
   chopped

MONTPELLIER BUTTER

Ingredients

8 Tbsp (1 stick) sweet
    butter, softened
1/4 cup extra virgin olive
    oil
1 oz Spanish anchovy,
    chopped
1 hard-cooked egg,
    chopped
1/4 Tbsp ground black
    pepper
2 Tbsp chevril, chopped
1 tsp garlic, chopped
1 tsp shallots chopped

ABOUT 1 CUP

Mix soft butter, olive oil, egg, black pepper,
chevril and anchovy.

Spread the butter over the warm fish it so
beautifully enhances as it melts.

MOUSSELINE SAUCE

ABOUT 2 CUPS

Melt butter and keep it warm.

In the top part of a double boiler, whisk egg yolks briskly until they begin to thicken.

Very slowly blend in the melted, warm butter.

Add the lemon juice and white wine.

Add salt.

When sauce is well combined and thickened, fold in whipped cream.

Mix well and keep warm until ready to use.

Ingredients

1/2 cup sweet butter
3 egg yolks, at room
  temperature
1 Tbsp fresh lemon juice
1 Tbsp dry white wine
1/4 tsp salt
1 cup heavy cream,
  whipped

OYSTER BAR
HOUSE DRESSING

Ingredients

1/2 cup olive oil
1/2 cup corn oil
1 Tbsp white vinegar
1 Tbsp dry white wine
2 Tbsp Dijon mustard
1 tsp salt
freshly ground white
    pepper to taste
1 tsp Worcestershire sauce
dash of Tabasco sauce
2 egg yolks
1 cup light cream

ABOUT 1 1/2 CUPS

Mix all ingredients well but don't over mix.

Let stand for about 1 hour before serving.

PICCATA

ABOUT 1 1/2 cups

Remove skin, seeds, and membrane from the lemons and crush the remaining fruit.

In a sauté pan, combine the butter, the lemon, and capers at medium heat.

Stir constantly, until butter turns light brown.

Add white wine and cook another 30 seconds over high heat.

Ingredients

2 lemons
4 oz capers
8 Tbsp (1 stick) sweet
   butter in one piece
6 oz white wine

SAUCE PROVENÇALE

Ingredients

3 large fresh tomatoes,
    peeled and seeded
2 oz olive oil
3 cloves fresh garlic ,finely
    chopped
4 sprigs fresh parsley,
    finely chopped
salt and pepper to taste
2 shallots, chopped
2 Tbsp fresh basil,
    chopped

Peel fresh tomatoes. For easy peeling, first score an "X" mark on top and bottom of tomatoes. Dip tomatoes in boiling water for 30 seconds. Remove tomatoes and submerge into iced water The skin can now be removed easily.

Cut flesh of tomato and remove all seeds and chop and drain.

In a heavy skillet heat olive oil and add chopped garlic and shallots, being careful not to burn it.

Add chopped tomatoes, chopped parsle and basil, salt and pepper. Stir until mixed.

Cook *sauce Provençale* over low heat for 5 to 10 minutes.

SAUCE RÉMOULADE

ABOUT 1 1/2 CUPS

Thoroughly combine all ingredients.

Refrigerate for at least 2 hours before serving.

Ingredients

1 cup basic mayonnaise
(see p. 23)
1 tsp fresh parsley minced
1/2 tsp capers, freshly
chopped and drained
1 Tbsp cornichons or
gherkins, finely
chopped and drained
1 hard-cooked egg, finely
chopped
1/2 tsp fresh tarragon,
minced
1/2 tsp fresh chives, finely
sliced
1 Tbsp Dijon mustard
1/2 tsp Old Bay
Seasoning

WHITE WINE
(VIN BLANC)
CREAM SAUCE

Ingredients

Same as p. 8, except as
noted

ABOUT 2 1/2 CUPS

Follow Champagne Sauce recipe on page 8. Substitute
dry white wine for the Champgane

RED WINE
CREAM SAUCE

ABOUT 2 1/2 CUPS

Substitute a strong cabernet or Barolo for white wine
and follow directions for white wine cream sauce
(see p. 32).

Ingredients

See White Wine Cream
Sauce (p. 32)

RUSSIAN DRESSING
(à la Russe)
with Cognac

Ingredients

1 cup basic mayonnaise
   (see p. 23)
1/3 cup ketchup
1/4 cup cognac
2 Tbsp chives, chopped
salt and pepper to taste

ABOUT 1 1/2 CUPS

In a mixing bowl, combine all the ingredients and whisk together into a creamy sauce.

SAFFRON SAUCE

ABOUT 2 CUPS

In a small sauté pan, place white wine and saffron and cook for 2 minutes.

Add white wine sauce and cook for one more minute.

Ingredients

3 Tbsp white wine
1 tsp saffron
16 oz white wine cream
sauce (see p.32)

SHALLOT SAUCE

Ingredients

1/2 cup red wine vinegar
1/2 cup tarragon vinegar
2 shallots, finely chopped
    or minced
pinch of salt
dash of Tabasco sauce
2 Tbsp ground black
    pepper

ABOUT 1 CUP

Combine all ingredients and mix thoroughly.

NOTE
This is an excellent sauce for oysters on the half shell, since it heightens their natural flavor.

STROGANOFF SAUCE

ABOUT 3 CUPS

Combine and reduce by three-fourths the white wine, white vinega, shallots, parsley stems, whole peppercorns,and paprika.

Add to this mixture the demi-glace and reduce by one third. Strain and season to taste.

Add 2 Tbsp sour cream and bring to light simmer.

Ingredients

1 cup white wine
1/4 cup white wine
    vinegar
2 Tbsp shallots
8 parsley stems
2 tbsp sweet Hungarian
    paprika
1 Tbsp whole black
    peppercorns
2 cups rich demi-glace
    (see p. 42-43)
2 Tbsp sour cream

TARRAGON DRESSING

Ingredients
(6-8 servings)

1/4 cup tarragon vinegar
1/4 cup shallots, finely
   chopped
3 Tbsp fresh tarragon,
   chopped
salt and pepper to taste
1/2 cup olive oil

ABOUT 1 CUP

In a mixing bowl, combine tarragon vinegar, shallots, fresh tarragon, salt and pepper.

Slowly whisk in the olive oil, allowing the dressing to thicken.

Chill.

TARTAR SAUCE

ABOUT 1 1/4 CUPS

Thoroughly combine all ingredients and chill for at least 2 hours before serving.

NOTE
The sauce may be thinned with a few drops of fresh lemon juice if it's too thick.

Ingredients

1 cup basic mayonnaise
    (see p. 23)
1 small boiled potato,
    cold, peeled, and
    mashed
1 tsp fresh parsley, minced
1/2 tsp capers, finely
    chopped
1 Tbsp dill pickle, finely
    chopped and drained
salt to taste
freshly ground white
    pepper to taste
3 Tbsp Dijon mustard

TOMATO SAUCE

Ingredients

2 oz virgin olive oil
2 garlic cloves, crushed
    and then minced
3 small onions, minced
28 oz can crushed
    tomatoes in purée
3 sprigs parsley, finely
    chopped
1 Tbsp fresh basil,
    chopped
pinch cayenne pepper
salt and pepper to taste

ABOUT 3 CUPS

In a large saucepan, over low heat, first add the oil, then combine the garlic and shallots. Stir until all is coated.

Cook over moderate heat for 2 to 3 minutes, until the garlic is just turning brown.

Add the tomato purée and stir to combine all ingredients.

Add the parsley and basil and stir to combine.

Add pinch of cayenne pepper.

Simmer for about 20 minutes, or until the sauce has thickened to the right consistency.

Salt and pepper to taste.

Excess sauce may be refrigerated or frozen.

TONNATO SAUCE

ABOUT 3 CUPS

In food processor add mayonnaise, tuna, 1 Tbsp capers, red vinegar, 1 garlic clove, 4 anchovy filets, Worcestershire, Tabasco.

Process until smooth.

Ingredients

2 cups basic
   mayonnaise
   (see p. 23)
8 oz tuna, cooked
1 Tbsp capers
1 Tbsp red vinegar
1 garlic clove, whole
4 small anchovy fillets,
   whole
1/4 tsp
   Worcestershire
4 drops Tabasco sauce

VEAL STOCK AND DEMI-GLACE REDUCTION

Ingredients

1 cup dry white wine
2 Tbsp vegetable oil
5 lb meaty veal bones and
   knuckles or combination
   of veal and beef bones
2 medium onions, trimmed
   and quartered (do not
   peel)
2 carrots, peeled and
   chopped
2 celery stalks, chopped
1 leek, halved lengthwise,
   and coarsely chopped
4 garlic cloves (do not
   peel)
1 small bunch parsley
   stems
2 cups water, plus more as
   needed
2 ripe fresh or canned
   tomatoes, cored and
   coarsely chopped
3 branches fresh thyme or
   1/2 tsp, dried
2 bay leaves
1/4 tsp coarse salt

MAKES ABOUT 3 QUARTS

Preheat oven to 450 F. Put oil in roasting pan, add bones and toss to coat. Roast 35 minutes.

Remove from oven. Add onions, carrots, celery, leek, garlic, and parsley stems, tossing with a wooden spoon to coat with fat.

Roast 30 minutes longe or until brown.

Remove pan from oven and transfer bones and vegetables to clean stockpot.

Drain off as much fat as possible from liquid left in the roasting pan. A good way to do this is to pour the liquid into a fat separator.

Place roasting pan over medium-high heat (use 2 burners if necessary), and add 2 cups cold water and boil briefly, scraping up all browned bits.

Transfer liquid to stockpot and add enough cold water to cover.

Bring slowly to boil, regularly skimming off all froth possible .

Lower heat and add wine, tomatoes, thyme, bay leaves, cloves, and salt.

Simmer uncovered 6 to 8 hours, adding water as needed just to cover ingredients; skim when necessary.

Strain into a large bowl, through a colander lined with double layer of dampened cheesecloth. Gently press solids to extract all liquids. Discard solids.

Cool to room temperature and refrigerate.

When the stock is chilled, lift off solidified fat and discard. Pour stock into containers for storage.

Label and date. Stock keeps 3 days in refrigerator, 6 months in freezer.

TO MAKE VEAL DEMI-GLACE REDUCTION

Boil 1/2 cup veal stock until very syrupy and reduced to about 2 tablespoons.

VINAIGRETTE
(Basic)

Ingredients

1 cup olive oil
1/2 cup balsamic vinegar
salt and pepper to taste

ABOUT 1 1/2 CUPS

Mix all ingredients together in a bowl.

VINAIGRETTE
(Mustard)

ABOUT 2 CUPS

Whisk all ingredients briskly into a creamy sauce.

In your refrigerator, preserve for future use whatever amount you have not used in your particular recipe.

Ingredients

1/4 cup white vinegar
1/2 cup dry white wine
3/4 cup olive oil
3/4 cup corn oil
2 tsp Dijon or Dusseldorf
     mustard
2 tsp salt
freshly ground white
     pepper to taste
1 tsp oregano
dash of Tabasco sauce
1 tsp Worcestershire
2 garlic cloves, finely
     chopped
1 tsp fresh parsley, finely
     chopped
1 small onion, minced

- SOUPS
- CHOWDERS
- STEWS
- PAN ROASTS

BOUILLABAISSE

Ingredients

FOR THE FISH STOCK

2 lb fish trimmings (heads, bones, etc,)
6 cups water
2 cups dry white wine

FOR THE BOUILLABAISSE

1/4 cup olive oil
1 large onion (about 1 cup), coarsely chopped
1/2 cup leeks, chopped (or chopped green onions may be used)
4–5 garlic cloves, minced
4 cups fish stock (see recipe)
4 medium-large tomatoes (about 1 1/2 cups), peeled and chopped
1 Tbsp salt, or to taste
1 Tbsp fresh fennel, chopped, or 1 1/2 tsp crushed fennel seeds
1 tsp grated orange rind
1 bay leaf
1/2–1 tsp saffron threads

FOR THE FISH STOCK

2 cups dry white wine. Cook for about 30 minutes.

Reduce heat and simmer until about 1 qt or half the original amount, of liquid is left. Strain, clarify, and reserve for use in the bouillabaisse.

FOR THE BOUILLABAISSE

In a large, heavy kettle or Dutch oven with a lid, heat the olive oil. Add onion, leeks, and garlic, and sauté for about 5 minutes.

Stir in fish stock, tomatoes, and all other seasonings, and bring to a boil.

Add clams and cover the kettle tightly. Boil for 2 or 3 minutes until the clams open. Remove clams from the broth with a slotted spoon, and set aside.

Reduce heat and add the fish and the scallops or shrimp so they are completely covered with the broth. Set clams back on top of fish.

Cover the kettle tightly once again and simmer the bouillabaisse over low heat for about 10 minutes, or until the fish is opaque and flakes easily with a fork.

Season to taste with salt and freshly ground black pepper. Ladle the broth over a toast slice in individual preheated bowls.

FOR THE *ROUILLE*

If you have a mortar and pestle, mash garlic and red peppers into a smooth paste. Otherwise mince and crush them until smooth.

Add rest of ingredients.

Aarrange fish on top with a slotted spoon and garnish with 1 Tbsp of rouille.

Sprinkle with croutons before serving.

Ingredients (cont'd)

1/2 tsp freshly ground
   black pepper, or to taste
1 dozen littleneck clams,
   well scrubbed, drained,
   and in the shell
1 1/2–2 lb firm white fish
   (halibut, haddock, cod
   or pollack), cut into
   serving pieces
1 lb bay scallops, or 1 lb
   fresh shrimp, peeled,
   deveined, and rinsed
salt to taste
freshly ground black
   pepper to taste
4 slices hot toast croutons
FOR THE *ROUILLE*
1 large red potato,
   peeled,and overcooked
4 cloves garlic, mashed or
   minced
2 red peppers or
   pimientos mashed or
   minced
1 cup mayonnaise (p. 23)

RED SNAPPER SOUP

Ingredients

2 Tbsp (1/4 stick) sweet
    butter
1 Tbsp flour
1 large onion (about 1
    cup), coarsely chopped
6 large tomatoes (about
    2–2 1/2 cups), peeled
    and coarsely chopped
1 clove garlic, minced
1 bay leaf
1 Tbsp fresh parsley,
    minced
1/4 tsp thyme
1/4 tsp sweet basil
3 cups water
4 red snapper fillets
    (about 2 lb total)
salt to taste
freshly ground white
    pepper to taste
3/4 cup dry white wine

SERVES 4-6

Melt butter in a large, heavy kettle.

Blend in flour and stir constantly until browned over low heat.

Add onion and cook until just tender, stirring constantly.

Add tomatoes and all seasonings to the kettle, and cook for a few minutes over low heat until tomatoes are soft.

Add water and bring all ingredients just to a boil.

Sprinkle snapper fillets with salt and pepper.

Add fish to the tomato mixture; reduce heat and simmer gently for about 15 minutes.

Add wine and bring mixture just to a boil again.

Reduce heat and simmer for 15 minutes more.

Serve one snapper fillet in each soup bowl with the broth.

SOUTH CAROLINA SHE-CRAB SOUP

SERVES 4

Melt butter in the top part of a double boiler over rapidly boiling water.

Stir in onion and sauté for 1 or 2 minutes until tender. Add crabmeat and roe.

Whisk yolks briskly in a bowl with salt, pepper, paprika, cayenne, Worcestershire, and parsley.

Blend yolks into the crabmeat and slowly add warm milk and half-and-half or light cream, stirring constantly.

Reduce heat and cook slowly over hot water for about 15 minutes, stirring occasionally with a wooden spoon.

Add a dollop of whipped cream (optional) to each serving, with a Tbsp of dry Sherry.

Ingredients

2 Tbsp (1/4 stick) sweet butter
1 small onion, minced
1 lb white female or "she-crab" crabmeat and roe, cooked and flaked
2 egg yolks
salt to taste
freshly ground white pepper to taste
dash of paprika
dash of cayenne
1/4 tsp Worcestershire sauce
1 Tbsp fresh parsley, minced
2 cups warm milk
1 1/2 cups half-and-half or light cream
1/2 cup heavy cream, whipped (optional)
4 Tbsp dry Sherry

CREAM OF SHRIMP SOUP

Ingredients

3/4 lb fresh shrimp, cooked, shelled, deveined, and finely chopped
1 cup half-and-half
2 Tbsp (1/4 stick) sweet butter
1 small onion, minced
1 or 2 stalks celery (about 1/2 cup), minced
1 Tbsp flour
1 tsp salt
1/2 tsp paprika
dash of freshly ground white pepper
1 tsp Worcestershire sauce
2 cups milk
1 cup heavy cream
2 Tbsp Sherry
1 Tbsp fresh parsley, minced

SERVES 4

Purée shrimp in a blender with half-and-half, and set aside.

Melt butter in the top part of a double boiler over boiling water.

Stir in onion and celery and cook for about 5 minutes until tender.

Blend in flour, salt, paprika, pepper, and Worcestershire.

Add shrimp purée, milk, and cream.

Cook over boiling water, stirring constantly until slightly thickened.

Stir in Sherry before serving.

Garnish with minced parsley.

NOTE
Finely chopped shrimp may be used as is instead of using the purée.

FISH CHOWDER

SERVES 4

Place haddock or cod fillets in a heavy kettle with bay leaf and 1 cup of the water.

Simmer over low heat until fish flakes easily with a fork.

Remove fish from the kettle with a slotted spoon, finish flaking, and set aside. Discard bay leaf.

Pour off fish stock and set aside.

Melt butter in the kettle and sauté onion over medium heat until golden.

Add flour and cook 2 minutes.

Add potatoes, celery, and remaining water to the kettle. Cover tightly and cook gently for about 12 minutes, or until potatoes and celery are tender.

Slowly stir in milk and cream (or half-and-half and milk).

Add fish and fish stock and heat just to boiling, stirring constantly.

Season with salt and pepper to taste.

Garnish with parsley.

Ingredients

3 Tbsp flour
1 lb haddock or cod fillets
1 bay leaf
2 cups water
2 Tbsp (1/4 stick) sweet butter
1 medium-large onion, finely chopped
2 medium raw potatoes (about 1 1/2 cups), peeled and diced
1 large stalk celery, minced
2 cups milk and 1 cup of light cream or 2 cups half-and-half and 1 cup milk
Salt to taste
dash of white pepper
1 Tbsp fresh parsley, minced

MANHATTAN CLAM CHOWDER

Ingredients

2 oz salt pork or slab bacon (rind removed), diced
1 pt fresh Quahog clams, removed from shell, and finely chopped
1/2 cups clam liquor or juice, strained
2 medium-large raw potatoes, peeled and diced
1/2 cup cold water
bouquet garni (see p. 11)
1 large onion, chopped
2 mediumleeks, choppedl
1 medium-large seeded green pepper, diced
1 or 2 stalks celery, diced
1 medium-large carrot, diced
1 Tbsp fresh parsley, minced
6 large tomatoes, peeled and chopped
1/4 cup tomato paste
1/4 cup tomato puree
1 tsp salt or to taste
dash of black peppe
5 dashesTobascor

SERVES 4

Sauté salt pork or bacon in a skillet until crisp and nicely browned.

Remove with a slotted spoon to a paper towel to drain.

Put salt pork or bacon and all other ingredients, including *bouquet garni*, in a large, heavy kettle, except clams.

Bring just to a boil; reduce heat and simmer, stirring occasionally, for about 45 minutes.

Add clams. Cool for 2 minutes.

Remove *bouquet garni* before serving chowder.

NEW ENGLAND CLAM CHOWDER

SERVES 4-6

Set shucked and finely chopped clams aside with strained (to remove any shell, etc.) clam juice.

Meanwhile, sauté salt pork or bacon in a skillet until crisp and nicely browned.

Remove with a slotted spoon to a paper towel to drain.

Sauté onion in the skillet for a few minutes until soft and translucent.

Add flour, and cook 5 minutes.

Add salt pork or bacon, onion, and clam juice to the potatoes and water. Bring just to a boil; reduce heat and simmer for10—15 minutes, until potatoes are tender.

Gradually stir milk and cream (or half-and-half and milk) into the kettle until hot, but not boiling.

Add clams and let them heat through for a minute or two. Season with salt and freshly ground white pepper to taste. Top with a pat of butter and a pinch of paprika to serve.

Ingredients

8 Tbsp flour
1 pt freshQuahog clams, opened, removed from shell, and finely chopped
1 1/2 cups clam juice, strained
2 cups water
2 medium-large raw potatoes (about 2 cups), peeled and diced
2 oz salt pork or slab bacon (rind removed), diced
1 large onion (about 1 cup), finely chopped
1 1/2 cups milk
1/2 cup light cream
1/2 tsp salt or to taste
dash of freshly ground white pepper
4 pats of sweet butter
pinch of paprika

NOTE. For a richer chowder, 2 cups half-and-half and 1/2 cup milk may be used instead.

CIOPPINO

Ingredients

3 oz corn oil
1 large onion, coarsely
    chopped
2 cloves garlic, minced
1 medium-large green
    pepper, finely chopped
4 medium-large tomatoes,
    peeled and coarsely
    chopped
1/2 cup tomato purée
1/4 cup Sherry
2 Tbsp tomato paste
1 bay leaf
1 tsp salt
generous sprinkling of fresh
    black pepper
2 Tbsp fresh parsley, minced
1/2–3/4 tsp oregano
pinch of basil
1 lb shrimp, shelled,
    deveined, and with tails
1/2 lb blackfin crabmeat,
    cooked
12 bay or sea scallops
1/2 lb haddock or cod
    fillets, cut in bite-size
    pieces
8 littleneck clams, in the
    shell

SERVES 4-6

Heat oil in a large, heavy kettle or Dutch oven.

Add onion, garlic, and green pepper, and sauté for about 5 minutes.

Stir in tomatoes, tomato purée, Sherry, tomato paste, and all the seasonings.

Simmer for about 1 hour, stirring occasionally.

Prepare the seafood.

Arrange shrimp, crabmeat, scallop and fish, with clams on top, in the tomato sauce.

Cover and cook over low heat for about 10 or 15 minutes until fish is opaque and clams are open.

Ladle into soup bowls and distribute the fish evenly to serve.

NOTE
If you prefer a thinner sauce, add a little water or, better still, fish stock, clam juice, etc., that has been set aside and reserved from recipe.

SHRIMP AND CRABMEAT GUMBO

SERVES 4-6

Heat oil to the smoking point.

Add flour and stir constantly until the roux is ruby red.

Add vegetables and cook 5 minutes.

Add seasoning.

Add rest of the ingredients except fish in a large, heavy kettle or oven.

Bring just to a boil.

Reduce heat and simmer for about 30 minutes.

Add shrimp and crab.

Simmer for about 5 minutes more.

Serve over rice pilaf and garnish with sliced scallions.

Ingredients

- 4 Tbsp flour
- 1 cup celery, chopped
- 1 lb fresh okra, washed, stems removed, and cut into 1-in pieces
- 1 large onion (about 1 cup), coarsely chopped
- 3 garlic cloves, minced
- 1/2 lb andouille sausage, diced
- 1 small green pepper, minced
- 1 bay leaf
- 1/2 tsp oregano
- 1 tsp salt, or to taste
- 1/2 tsp black pepper
- 1/2 tsp white pepper
- 1/2 tsp crushed red pepper
- 5 large tomatoes (about 2-2 1/2 cups), peeled and coarsely chopped
- 1/2 cup tomato sauce
- 1 1/2 cups fish stock
- 4 Tbsp corn oil
- 2 lb raw shrimp, peeled, deveined, rinsed
- 2 lb blackfin crabmeat, cooked
- 1/2 tsp cream

OYSTER STEW

Ingredients
(serves 1)

8 freshly opened oysters
2 Tbsp (1/4 stick) sweet
    butter
1/4 cup oyster liquor
dash of celery salt
1 tsp Worcestershire
1 oz of clam juice
1/2 tsp paprika
1 cup half-and-half

Place all ingredients, except half-and-half and 1 Tbsp of the butter, in the top part of a double boiler over boiling water. Don't let the top part of the boiler pan touch the water below.

Whisk briskly for about 1 minute, until oysters are just beginning to curl.

Add half-and-half and continue stirring briskly, just to a boil. Do not boil.

Pour stew into soup plate.

Serve piping hot topped with the remaining 1 Tbsp butter and sprinkle with paprika.

SERVES 6 OR MORE

In a large, heavy skillet, sauté garlic and onion in oil.

Add oregano and chicken breasts and brown nicely on both sides.

Remove chicken, garlic, and onions to a large, heavy kettle or Dutch oven.

Add tomatoes, salt and pepper to taste, parsley, chorizo or pepperoni, ham, rice, saffron, and water.

Bring all ingredients just to a boil.

Reduce heat and simmer for about 10 minutes.

Add shrimp and clams and continue cooking over low heat for about 10 minutes more, or until liquid is absorbed and the rice is tender.

Fluff rice with a fork, and taste to be sure it is cooked.

Clams should be open and the shrimp should be pink.

Sprinkle cooked green peas over the top.

Arrange pimientos attractively over all.

Ingredients

2 garlic cloves, minced
1 large onion (about 1 cup), coarsely chopped
1/4 cup olive oil
1 tsp oregano
2 lb boned chicken breasts with skin, cut in serving pieces
5 large tomatoes (about 2–2 1/2 cups), peeled and coarsely chopped
salt to taste
freshly ground black pepper
3 Tbsp fresh parsley, chopped
1 chorizo (hot Spanish sausage), cut in 1-in pieces
1/4 lb ham, diced
1 1/2 cups raw white rice
1 tsp saffron
2 cups water
1 lb shrimp, peeled and deveined
1 dozen littleneck clams, in the shell
1 cup fresh green peas, cooked
2 large pimientos, coarsely cut

WATERZOOI
(Belgian Fish Stew)

Ingredients

2 lb fish trimmings (heads, bones, etc.)
2 qt water
1 large onion (about 1 cup), coarsely chopped
1 stalk celery with leaves, coarsely chopped
1 bay leaf
2 cloves garlic, minced
1 medium carrot, coarsely chopped
1 tsp salt, or to taste
ground white pepper to taste
2 lb boneless striped bass cut in serving pieces
1 Tbsp fresh parsley minced croutons

SERVES 6-8

In a large, heavy saucepan boil the fish trimmings in water with onion, celery, bay leaf, garlic, carrot, salt, and pepper for about 30 minutes.

Reduce heat and simmer until 1 qt, or half the original amount, of liquid is left.

Strain liquid into a large, heavy kettle and discard the fish trimmings and vegetables.

Place striped bass in the kettle and completely cover with the broth.

Cook over very low heat until the striped bass is opaque and flakes easily with a fork.

Sprinkle with parsley and top with croutons before serving.

SOLIANKA
(Russian Sturgeon Stew)

Ingredients

SERVES 6

In a large, heavy saucepan boil the fish trimmings in water seasoned with salt and pepper for about 30 minutes.

Meanwhile, sauté tomatoes in a large, heavy kettle with the oil. Stir frequently until tomatoes form a smooth paste.

Add cutup fillets, onion, pickles, capers, and green olives to the kettle.

Strain the fish broth into the kettle and discard the fish trimmings.

Add the bay leaf and parsley.

Simmer over low heat for about 15–20 minutes.

Stir in butter and cook over low heat for another minute.

Top each serving with black olives, lemon, cucumber, and a sprig of parsley.

2 lb fish trimmings (heads, bones, etc.)
1 1/2 qt water
1 tsp salt
generous sprinkling of freshly ground white pepper
2 large tomatoes, peeled and coarsely chopped
1/4 cup corn oil
1 lb sturgeon fillets, cut in four serving pieces
1 large onion (about 1 cup), coarsely chopped
2 dill pickles, coarsely chopped
1 Tbsp capers
1 Tbsp pitted green olives, coarsely chopped
1 bay leaf
1 Tbsp fresh parsley, chopped
4 Tbsp (1/2 stick) sweet butter
1 Tbsp pitted black olives, thinly sliced
1 lemon, thinly sliced
1 medium cucumber, peeled, halved, seeded, and thinly sliced

OYSTER PAN ROAST

Ingredients
(serves 1)

8 freshly opened oysters
2 Tbsp (1/4 stick)
    sweet butter
1 Tbsp chili sauce
1 Tbsp Worcestershire
    sauce
1/4 cup oyster liquor
1/2 tsp paprika
dash of celery salt
1 oz of clam juice
1/2 cup cream
1 slice dry toast

Place all ingredients except cream, toast, and 1 Tbsp of the butter in the top part of a double boiler over boiling water. Don't let the top pan of the double boiler touch the water below.

Whisk or stir briskly and constantly for about 1 minute, until oysters are just beginning to curl.

Add cream and continue stirring briskly. Do not boil.

Pour pan roast into a soup plate over the slice of dry toast.

Top with remaining 1 Tbsp butter, and sprinkle with paprika.

NOTE
To create other individual stews and pan roasts, simply substitute for the oysters the following ingredients:

shrimp: 8 raw shrimp, shelled, deveined, with tails off
clams: 8 freshly opened cherrystone or littleneck clams
lobster : 2 oz fresh lobster meat
scallops:10–12 raw bay scallop
mussels:14–16, bearded, but in the shell.
mixture: 3 shrimp, 2 oysters, 2 clams, 3 scallops, 2 oz lobster

EGG DISHES

CRÊPES

Ingredients

2 eggs
3/4 cup all-purpose flour
1/2 tsp salt
1 tsp baking powder
2/3 cup milk
1/3 cup heavy cream
vegetable oil

MAKES 12–14 CRÊPES

Place all dry ingredients in a large mixing bowl. Make a wel, pour in liquid ingredients. Combine them with a whisk. Add a few drops of oil.

Refrigerate at least 3 hours.

Heat a 5-inch crêpe skillet. Grease it with 2 or 3 drops of oil. Add a small quantity of crêpe batter.

Before the batter settles, tip the skillet, allowing the batter to spread and cover the bottom.

When the crêpe is brown underneath, turn and brown other side. Use a few drops of oil in skillet before cooking each pancake.

NOTE
Never stack crêpes one on top of the other without separating them first with a sheet of wax paper.

BAKED BRUNCHEON EGGS

SERVES 4

Remove the yolks from the shelled and split hard-cooked eggs and mash them with a fork. Set the whites aside.

Melt sweet butter in a medium sized heavy saucepan or skillet.

Add the onion and cook over low heat until tender.

Add the mushrooms and sauté them until tender.

Stir in crabmeat, cream, parsley, salt and pepper, mustard, paprika, and mashed egg yolks.

Combine thoroughly, and stuff egg whites with the mixture.

Arrange the stuffed eggs in an ovenproof serving dish. Spoon the egg sauce over all and sprinkle Parmesan cheese on top.

Bake for 4 or 5 minutes until heated through.

Place the eggs briefly under the broiler to brown lightly before serving.

NOTE
The eggs with sauce may be served in a rice mold or on toast points.

Ingredients

8 hard-cooked eggs, shelled and cut in half
2 Tbsp (1/4 stick) sweet butter
1 small onion, minced
1/4 lb mushrooms with stems, finely chopped
1/4 cup blackfin crabmeat, cooked
1/4 cup heavy cream
Tbsp fresh parsley, finely chopped
salt to taste
freshly ground white pepper to taste
pinch of dry mustard
pinch of paprika
2 cups egg sauce
(see p. 13)
1/4 cup Parmesan cheese, grated

EGGS BENEDICT
Finnan Haddie
(Smoked Haddock)

Ingredients

4 English muffins, split and
   toasted
3 Tbsp sweet butter
3/4 lb finnan haddie,
   thinly sliced on an
   angle
8 poached eggs
   (see p. 69)
1 cup basic Hollandaise
   sauce (see p. 20)
paprika

SERVES 4

Split and toast English muffins.

Melt butter in a medium-sized heavy skillet, and sauté finnan haddie slices until lightly brown and crispy.

Top each muffin half with a slice of finnan haddie. Slide muffins under broiler flame for 1 minute.

Remove from broiler and top each muffin half with a freshly poached egg.

Spoon 2 Tbsp Hollandaise sauce over each egg.

Sprinkle with paprika and serve immediately

EGGS BENEDICT
with Smoked Salmon

SERVES 4

Toast English muffins. Place two slices smoked salmon on each half English muffin.

Set aside in warm place. Poach eggs.

TO POACH EGGS
In a small sauce pot, bring water to a boil, and add vinegar.

Have ready 8 eggs. When the water is coming to a boil, drop in the eggs, reduce the heat until water is quiet, and simmer 4 minutes. The egg whites should be firm and the yolk soft.

Remove eggs with a skimmer or slotted spoon. Drain well.

Place one poached egg on top of salmon and each half English muffin and cover with Hollandaise sauce.

Serve hot at once.

Ingredients

4 English muffins split in half
16 slices smoked salmon sliced thin
4 cups water
1/4 cup distilled vinegar
8 large eggs
basic Hollandaise sauce (p. 20)

EGGS MADISON

Ingredients

4 English muffins, split and
   toasted
1/4 cup anchovy butter
   (see p. 4)
8 thin slices smoked
   salmon, preferably lox
8 poached eggs
   (see p. 69)
1 cup basic Hollandaise
   sauce (see p. 20)
capers (optional)

SERVES 4

Split and toast English muffins.

Spread each half with anchovy butter.

Top each muffin with a slice of salmon and a poached egg.

Spoon Hollandaise sauce over the eggs before serving.

Sprinkle capers over the top of all (optional).

SERVES 4

Roll oysters in flour, coating well.

Dip oysters into the 2 eggs and then into cracker crumbs.

Melt butter in a large, heavy skillet until just sizzling but not brown.

Add oysters and brown quickly on each side, but be careful not to overcook.

Meanwhile, beat the 6 eggs in a bowl with the half-and-half, season with salt and pepper and pour over oysters in the skillet.

Reduce heat and cook until eggs are set and the underneath begins to brown nicely.

Fold omelette over carefully with a spatula into a half circle, and lift onto a prewarmed platter.

Top each serving with a strip of bacon.

Serve with cocktail sauce (optional).

Ingredients

1 pt oysters, shucked and drained (reserve oyster liquor and set aside for another use)
1/2 cup all-purpose flour
2 eggs, beaten well
1 cup soda crackers or saltines, finely crushed
8 Tbsp (1 stick) sweet butter
6 eggs
1/4 cup half-and-half
salt to taste
freshly ground white pepper to taste
4 slices bacon, broiled or fried crisp
1 cup cocktail sauce (see p. 9)

SHRIMP NEWBURG OMELETTE

Ingredients

4 individual or 1 large
 omelette for 4 persons
 (see p. 73)
4 Tbsp (1/2 stick) sweet
 butter
1 lb shrimp, cooked,
 shelled, deveined, and
 coarsely chopped
1/4 cup Dry Sack wine
dash of paprika
1 cup heavy cream
3 egg yolks
salt to taste
freshly ground white
 pepper to taste
1 Tbsp fresh parsley,
 minced

Melt butter in the top part of a double boiler.

Add shrimp and cook over boiling water for about 1 or 2 minutes.

Stir in wine and continue cooking and stirring for 2 minutes.

Whisk the paprika and cream together.

Whisk in the egg yolks and add the cream mixture to the shrimp.

Stir until smooth and the Newburg begins to thicken. Don't let the Newburg boil and don't let the top part of the double boiler sit in the water.

Season with salt and pepper.

Spoon most of the shrimp Newburg onto the omelette(s) and fold over, adding more Newburg on top of the omelette (see p. 73).

Sprinkle with parsley before serving.

RED CAVIAR OMELETTE

SERVES 3-4

TO MAKE OMELETTE

In a bowl, briskly whisk eggs, cream, salt, pepper, onion, and parsley.

Melt butter in a medium-sized heavy skillet or omelette pan over medium heat.

Swish butter around the skillet until it's thoroughly coated and butter is almost sizzling.

Pour in egg mixture and reduce heat.

Lift the sides and underneath of the omelette with a spatula as the eggs begin to set.

TO MAKE RED CAVIAR OMELETTE

When eggs are set but slightly moist in the center, place caviar on one side of the omelette, fold over the other half and lift the omelette gently with a spatula to a prewarmed platter.

Ingredients
(each serving can use a 2
or 3–egg option)

6 eggs
2 Tbsp heavy cream
1/2 tsp salt
dash of freshly ground
white pepper
1 tsp onion, minced
1 tsp fresh parsley, minced
6 Tbsp (3/4 stick) sweet
butter
1/2 cup red caviar (or
black if you want to
splurge)

WESTERN
TUNA OMELETTE

Ingredients

2 Tbsp olive oil
1 medium onion, coarsely
   chopped
1 medium green pepper,
   coarsely chopped
8 eggs
3/4 lb tuna, cooked,
   drained, and flaked (or
   canned tuna
   may be used)
1/2 tsp salt
dash of freshly ground
   white pepper

SERVES 4

Heat oil in a medium-sized heavy skillet. Add onion, green pepper.

Cook over low heat until vegetables are just tender, about 5 minutes.

Whisk eggs briskly in a bowl until they begin to get thick and creamy.

Stir in tuna, salt, and peppe and vegetables.

Pour eggs, tuna and vegetables into the skillet.

Cook over medium heat, lifting the edges with a spatula and tilting the skillet to let soft eggs run underneath.

When eggs are slightly browned underneath and set on top, turn onto a prewarmed platter. Do not fold.

NOTE
The omelette may be cut in wedges as a pie, and served on toast points spread lightly with mayonnaise (see p. 23) that has been sprinkled with fresh lemon juice.

HADDOCK SOUFFLÉ

INDIVIDUAL SERVING

Preheat oven to 350 F.

Melt butter in a large, heavy saucepan. Slowly blend in flour, salt, pepper, and cayenne over low heat.

Add half-and-half and continue stirring constantly over low heat until mixture is smooth and begins to thicken.

Separate eggs and set whites aside. Add egg yolks to cream mixture, one at a time, mixing thoroughly after each yolk is added. Bring mixture just to boiling.

Remove from heat and add the cooked and flaked fish.

Set fish mixture aside and let cool. Meanwhile, beat egg whites until they are stiff.

Fold whites into the fish mixture and mix gently but well.

Pour into lightly buttered casserole (1–1 1/2-qt) and bake for 40–45 minutes until the soufflé is firm and puffy.

NOTE
Cod, flounder or other white fish fillets may be substituted for haddock. The soufflé may also be topped with cheddar cheese.

Ingredients

3 Tbsp sweet butter
3 Tbsp flour
1/2 tsp salt
dash of ground white
    pepper
pinch of cayenne
1 cup half-and-half
3 eggs
1 lb haddock fillets,
    cooked and flaked

SHELLFISH

SHELLFISH

The term shellfish includes both crustacea and mollusks. Since they all taste so much better than these two names would indicate, we'll mention only briefly that oysters, clams, mussels, and scallops are bivalve mollusks with two valves that open and close. Crustacea, as their name implies, are covered with a crust-like thin shell and you know them as shrimp, lobster, and crab.

It's easier to shop for shellfish than for regular fish, since you have to look for only one thing. Nature has thoughtfully provided the signs that mean shellfish is fresh—and done it in reverse for each species. Oysters, clams, mussels, and scallops like privacy, and they're alive and fresh only when their shells are tightly closed. Never buy one that has even a slightly gaping shell. Shrimp, lobsters, and crabs are the extroverts, and the livelier the movement of their claws and eyes the fresher they're likely to be.

CLAMS

Buying and understanding what you're buying, can be a puzzling experience for anyone new to purchasing clams because there's such a variety of them. All clams are related, but each one is different from its relatives in some special way. It's that difference which will determine what type of clam will become your own special favorite, and while you're experimenting, you'll have an adventure in fine eating.

The most familiar clams on the East Coast are either soft or hard. Soft clams are the ones with the long hose-like neck. They're also called steamers. The soft clam is ideally suited for steaming, and it's a staple of any shore or Landlubbers' Clambake (see p. 86). It's also good for any recipe that calls for chopped clams, and many people prefer soft clams to hard for making a chowder. Soft shell crabs are also perfect for shucking and frying.

New Englanders insist there is no finer clam—except perhaps the quahog, the Indian name for the hard clam. You'll buy hard clams under three different names, depending on their size. The largest hard clam is called a chowder clam. The medium size is a cherrystone. The smallest one is the littleneck. Cherrystones and littlenecks are most often served ice cold on the half shell with Cocktail Sauce (see p. 9) or just a few drops of fresh lemon juice and coarsely ground black pepper. There are chefs who will use only one or the other for clam chowder. Since these hard clams are so adaptable, you can use them however you choose to in any recipe. There are so many varieties of clams on the Pacific Coast that we'll mention only the famous Pismo and razor clams that occasionally turn up in Eastern restaurants and fish stores.

You can buy clams in their shells by the dozen, or shucked by the pint or quart. For a feast there are pecks and bushels available. Six clams on the half shell are usually served for 1 person, although a dozen is not unusual, depending on one's appetite. A pint of shucked clams with their juice will generally serve 4 persons if other ingredients are used in the recipe. If in doubt, it's best to buy a quart. All clams have one thing in common: they're sandy and must be washed very well. Nothing can destroy the enjoyment of eating clams quicker than finding a few grains of sand in one of them.

TO CLEAN SOFT CLAMS
Scrub clams thoroughly with a stiff brush in cold water. Rinse them well in 4 or 5 changes of cold water.

Put clams in a large kettle and cover with cold water.

Add 1 cup cornmeal to the clams and let them stand for 8 hours. This is called "floating." Immediately discard any clam that floats. Rinse well in cold running water.

Clams are ready to be steamed or opened.

TO COOK SOFT CLAMS
Place clams with 1 cup water in a large heavy kettle or Dutch oven. Add 1 tsp salt and cover the kettle/Dutch oven.

Steam over low heat for about 6 or 7 minutes, or just until the clams open.
Clams are ready to serve.

NOTE
See Steamed Clams with Broth and Drawn Butter (p. 91).

TO CLEAN HARD CLAMS
Chowder clams: same as cheerystones and littlenecks.
Scrub clams thoroughly with a stiff brush under cold running water. Discard any clams with broken or gaping shells. Clams are ready to be opened.

TO COOK HARD CLAMS
For steaming open: same as soft clams.

On the half shell or for other dishes:
Hold clam in the palm of your left hand with the shell hinge (or round, lip part) facing you. Insert a thin, strong, and sharp knife between the shells (if you don't have a clam opener or an oyster knife—both good investments).
Push the knife in and twist it sharply left and right to sever the clam's heavy muscle. Remove the top shell.

Cut the remaining muscle close to the lower shell, and loosen the clam, being careful to retain its juice.

CLAM CROQUETTES

Ingredients

1 pt clams, opened, drained, removed from shell, and finely chopped (reserve clam juice)
1 tsp salt
sprinkling of freshly ground white pepper
pinch of paprika
1 small onion, minced
4 Tbsp all-purpose flour
2 Tbsp (1/2 stick) sweet butter
1/2 cup half-and-half
1 egg, well beaten
1 hard-cooked egg, finely chopped
1 egg, beaten
1 cup fine bread crumbs
peanut oil for deep frying

SERVES 3-4

Put clams in a bowl and season with salt, pepper, and paprika. Mix in onion. Set aside.

Thoroughly blend flour, butter, half-and-half, and well-beaten egg over boiling water in the top part of a double boiler.

Cook, stirring constantly, until the sauce thickens. Blend in clams and the hard-cooked egg.

Remove from heat and let the clam mixture cool thoroughly. When cool, roll the mixture into cone shapes.

Refrigerate the clam cones, covered, for 1 hour. Roll the croquettes/cones in beaten egg and then in crumbs, coating thoroughly.

Heat oil for deep frying to 375 F in a large heavy kettle or Dutch oven. A piece of bread dropped into the oil will turn golden brown when the temperature of the oil is just right.

Fry the croquettes until golden brown, about 3 to 5 minutes. Drain croquettes on paper towels. Good served with a favorite cream sauce.

CLAM FRITTERS

SERVES 3-4

Drain clams, and set juice aside for later use if necessary.

Thoroughly mix milk, pancake mix, cornmeal, salt, and pepper in a large bowl.

Gently fold the clams into the batter.

Heat oil and butter in a heavy 10-inch skillet until just sizzling.

Drop batter into the skillet by the tablespoonful.

Be sure that two clams are included with each tablespoonful.

Fry until golden brown on one side, about 2 minutes.

Turn each clam fritter carefully with tongs, and brown on the other side for about 2 minutes.

If batter becomes too thick while standing, thin it with a few spoonfuls of clam juice.

Reserve the remaining clam juice for another use. Drain fritters on a paper towel. Serve with lemon wedges or any favorite seafood sauce.

Ingredients

1 pt littleneck clams, opened, removed from shell, and with juice
1/2 cup evaporated milk
1 cup dry pancake mix
2 Tbsp cornmeal
1 tsp salt
generous sprinkling of ground black pepper
1 cup corn oil
2 Tbsp (1/4 stick) sweet butter

CLAM FRY

Ingredients

1 qt soft shelll clams,
  opened removed from
  shell, and drained. (Buy
  an extra pt for hearty
  appetites. Reserve clam
  juice for another use.)
1 tsp salt
generous sprinkling of
  freshly ground white
  pepper
1 cup flour
2 eggs, well beaten
1 tsp heavy cream
1 cup seasoned bread
  crumbs
8 Tbsp (1 stick) sweet
  butter
1 Tbsp corn oil
1 1/4 cup Tartar sauce
  (see p.39)
lemon wedges (optional)

SERVES 4-6

Season flour with salt and pepper.

Dip clams in flour and coat well.

Beat eggs and cream together until frothy.

Dip clams in egg mixture

Crumble crackers between sheets of waxed paper with
a rolling pin for fine crumbs.

Dip clams in crumbs and thoroughly coat.

Heat butter and oil in a large heavy skillet to just
sizzling. Do not brown or let the butter smoke.

Reduce heat a bit and drop clams into the hot butter.

Fry until golden brown, about 3 minutes.

Turn and fry for about 2 minutes on the other side.

Drain on paper towels.

Serve with Tartar sauce and wedges of lemon
(optional).

CLAMS CASINO

SERVES 4

Preheat oven to 450 F.

Place the tins with the rock salt in the oven.

Combine all ingredients except the bacon and clams in a large bowl, and mix well.

Top each clam with a spoonful of the mixture.

Top the mixture with a piece of bacon.

Remove tins from the oven and embed the clams firmly in the hot salt.

Return pans to the oven and bake until bacon is crisp, about 6 to 8 minutes.

Serve clams right in the tin.

Ingredients

4 pie or cake tins half filled with rock salt (or 1 baking pan large enough to hold the clams)

2 dozen clams, opened and on the half shell

8 Tbsp (1 stick) sweet butter, softened

1/2 cup shallots, minced (or scallions may be used instead)

1 pimiento, minced

1/2 cup green pepper, minced

3 Tbsp fresh parsley, minced

1 tsp salt or to taste

generous sprinkling of freshly ground black pepper

dash of Worcestershire sauce

dash of Tabasco sauce

2 Tbsp fresh lemon juice

6 slices bacon, each cut in four pieces

LANDLUBBERS' CLAMBAKE
(A Shore Dinner Indoors)

Ingredients

Plenty of damp seaweed (corn husks, celery, lettuce, or spinach leaves may be used instead)
1 huge pot, kettle, wash boiler, lard can (or any other container large enough to steam the feast), with a lid
1 qt water
4 1 1/4 to 1 1/2 lb lobsters
4 ears of corn, husks on
4 dozen soft clams (see instructions for cleaning on p. 81)

1–1 1/2 lb (4–6 sticks) sweet butter, melted

SERVES 4

Cover the bottom of the container (pot, kettle, etc.) with about 3 to 4 inches of damp seaweed or corn husks, etc.

Add 1 qt water and turn up the heat on your stove until the water boils.

Place lobsters in the container and cover them with a layer of seaweed/corn husks, etc.

Add foil-wrapped corn ears on top of the lobsters and cover them with another layer of seaweed/corn husks.

Place clams on top of the corn and cover with more seaweed/corn husks, etc. Reduce heat to medium.

Cook 15–20 minutes.

The clambake is ready.

Now comes the best part.

On the table have preheated bowls of hot melted butter
salt, pepper mill, 24 large white paper napkins,
4 paper bibs (festive for the mood of the clambake,
and usually decorated with a lobster), 4 nutcrackers, or
heavy-handled and dull knives (for lobsters), 4 soup
bowls (for the clams), 4 serving platters (for
everything).

Turn heat off under the container.

Lift clams from the container with a ladle into the soup
bowls, retaining as much juice as possible.

When clams have been eaten, discard shells.

Remove ears of corn from the container with tongs.
Take lobsters from the container with tongs, and serve
on the individual platters.

NOTE
A plain white and easy-to-wipe vinyl tablecloth is
highly recommended for indoor clambakes.

TRADITIONAL NEW ENGLAND CLAMBAKE
(Outdoors At The Shore)

You'll need:

Piles of rocks
Charcoal (if the supply of
    rocks is limited)
Plenty of driftwood and
    any other non-treated
    available wood
Plenty of seaweed
4 2 to 2 1/2 lb lobsters
8 dozen soft clams
1 canvas tarpaulin
1 1/2 l, (4–6 sticks)
    sweet butter, melted in
    a foil or other fireproof
    container
potato chips (bag version)

SERVES 8 OR MORE

Dig a large hole in the sand and line it with rocks and charcoal. Put the largest rocks on the bottom.

 Get a good bonfire going with driftwood and any other wood you can pick up on the beach. Heap more rocks and charcoal on the fire.

When the fire has burned for about 2 hours, or the rocks are steaming and the charcoal is a fiery red, cover all with the first thin layer of seaweed.

Place the lobsters on top of the seaweed, and cover them with another layer of seaweed. Put half the clams on top of the lobsters and cover them with a layer of seaweed.

Add the remaining clams and cover them with a thick 4 or 5 inch layer of seaweed.

Put a canvas tarpaulin over all, and secure it with heavy rocks. Bake for about 20 minutes, or until the clams begin to open.

Butter, melted in "roughing it" do-it-yourself containers (including well-scrubbed cans), is a concession—but a tasty one that adds to the enjoyment of both clams and lobsters!

Serve potato chips as a side dish.

SOFTSHELL CLAMS
Fried In Rice Batter
with Tartar Sauce

SERVES 4-6

Shuck and clean clams, pat dry.

Place clams in rice flour and shake off excess.

Deep fry at 375 F for 2–3 minutes or until lightly browned.

Serve with Tartar sauce.

Ingredients

2 lb freshly shucked clams,
   necks removed
1 lb rice flour
1 egg, beaten
8 oz Tartar sauce (p. 39).

STEAMED SOFTSHELL CLAMS
with Clam Broth and Drawn Butter

Ingredients

8 lbs softshell clams
  (steamers)
1 1/2 cup white wine
2 stalks celery, cut into
  2-in pieces
8 oz drawn sweet butter

SERVES 4-6

Bring clams, white wine and celery to boil and simmer for 5–8 minutes, depending on size of clams.

Serve with broth and melted butter in separate small bowls for dipping.

STEAMED CLAMS
with Broth
and Drawn Butter

Place clams in a large heavy kettle or Dutch oven.

Add onion, garlic, wine, and pepper.

Cover tightly and steam just until the clams open.

If any of the clams don't open, discard them immediately.

Remove the clams with a slotted spoon to individual serving bowls or one large serving dish.

Strain broth and discard onion and garlic.

Serve cups of clam broth and hot melted butter on the side.

Ingredients

6 dozen hardshell clams in the shell
1 large onion, minced
3 large cloves garlic, minced
1 cup dry white wine
generous sprinkling of freshly ground white pepper
1 lb (4 sticks) sweet butter, melted

BAKED STUFFED CLAMS

Ingredients

4 pie or cake tins half
   filled with rock salt (or
   1 baking pan large
   enough to hold the
   clams)
2 dozen clams
1 small onion, minced
1 Tbsp garlic, minced
1 Tbsp fresh parsley,
   minced
3 Tbsp sweet butter,
   melted
1/2 cup fine bread
   crumbs

SERVES 4

Preheat oven to 400 F.

Place the tins with the rock salt in the oven.

Remove clams from their shells, and reserve 24 halfshells.

Reserve clam liquor and set aside.

Chop the clams very fine and combine in a bowl with onion and parsley and garlic.

Mix 1 Tbsp melted butter and bread crumbs and add to the clams.

Melt the remaining 2 Tbsp of butter in a small, heavy saucepan. Add flour and stir over low heat until well blended.

Pour in clam liquor and stir until the mixture is smooth.

Gradually blend in half-and-half and continue cooking over low heat for about 5 minutes, stirring constantly until thickened.

Add Sherry, salt, pepper, and paprika.

Thoroughly mix cream sauce in the bowl with the clams. Spoon mixture into the clam shells and dot with the remaining butter.

Remove tins from the oven and embed the clams firmly in the hot salt. Return pans to the oven and bake until the tops of the clams are nicely browned.

Garnish with lemon wedges.

Ingredients (cont'd)

2 Tbsp (1/4 stick) sweet butter
1 1/2 Tbsp all-purpose flour
1/2 cup half-and-half
1 Tbsp Sherry
1 tsp salt
sprinkling of freshly ground white pepper
pinch of paprika
2 Tbsp (1/4 stick) sweet butter
4 lemons, cut in wedges

CRABS

There's only one way to eat a hard-shell or blue crab and that's to cover the table with newspapers or brown paper, forget about all utensils except a wooden mallet or a dull table knife (the handle is ideal for cracking claws), and go to work! The blue crab is found along the Atlantic Coast from Cape Cod to Florida, but from April to December the Chesapeake Bay provides more blue crabs than any other body of water in the world. Aside from live blue crabs, which are sold by the dozen, cooked crabmeat is picked fresh and sold by the pound in many seafood markets, and also commercially shipped fresh in iced containers.

Crabmeat has an exquisite and distinctive flavor totally unlike any other shellfish. Lump backfin is white meat taken from the body of the crab; the claw meat is a brownish color but just as choice. Flaked crabmeat is also sold, and it's perfect for soups and other dishes that don't require larger pieces of crab. Allow at least 6 hard-shell crabs per person when serving steamed crabs. One pound of cooked crabmeat is usually sufficient for most dishes that will serve 4 persons. The Oyster Bar sets aside a special week every year during which a real crab feast is served that you can easily duplicate at home. The menu begins with South Carolina She-crab Soup (see p.51) and moves up the coast to Maryland for Steamed Crabs (see p. 95), Crab Cakes (see p.96), Crab Imperial (see p.97), etc.

Other types of crabs, such as Florida stone crabs, Alaskan king crab legs, Dungeness crabs from the Pacific Coast, and soft-shell crabs, are served throughout the year as they become available. At the same time you may be able to find these varieties of crab in your local markets. Many people don't realize that the soft crab is really the same hard-shell or blue crab caught right after shedding its hard shell, which it does many times before reaching maturity. To add to the confusion, the crab in its soft and molted state has an entirely different taste from the "other life" hard-shell crab. It also has no claws, so that when the soft-shell crab is sautéed or broiled all of the crab with its firm white meat is eaten. The flavor defies description! When buying soft-shell crabs allow 2 for each person and a word of advice— have your market clean them for you. At home in the kitchen, it's work—and not entirely pleasant. The peak of the soft-shell crab season is July and August.

TO STEAM HARD-SHELL CRABS
1/2 cup Old Bay seasoning

2 cups white vinegar
2 cups beer (or water)
2 dozen live and lively blue crabs

Thoroughly mix the seafood seasoning and salt with the vinegar and beer (or water).

Put 1 dozen of the crabs in a huge steamer or pot with a rack and a tight-fitting lid. Pour half the seasoning over the crabs.

Add the remaining 1 dozen crabs and pour the rest of the seasoning over them. Cover the steamer or pot tightly and steam the crabs, using the beer and vinegaras liquid, over medium high heat for about 20 minutes until the crabs turn bright red.

Remove from steamer and serve hot immediately.

The crabs need no sauce or additional seasoning, but at an authentic Crab Feast small bowls of vinegar are served on the side to be sprinkled over the crabmeat, along with a pepper mill for freshly ground black pepper.

If the crabs are to be served cold, or the meat picked from them for another dish, they should cool at room temperature before being refrigerated. Be sure that all cartilage has been removed from the picked crabmeat to avoid a sensation not unlike finding a grain of sand in a clam!

TO PICK A HARD-SHELL CRAB
Place crab on its back. Remove tail flap. With both hands crack shell in half (it should break open readily). Meat may now be extracted from shell with aid of a spoon. Avoid stomach and mouth; they may be removed by pressing thumbs down on mouth until it breaks away from shell. Break off claws and legs with a heavy knife or a wooden mallet.

CRAB CAKES

Ingredients

1 egg
2 Tbsp mayonnaise
(see p. 23)
1 tsp lemon juice
1/2 tsp Dijon mustard
1 Tbsp Worcestershire
sauce
generous dash of Old Bay
seasoning
1 lb fresh crab meat
2 Tbsp fresh parsley,
minced
2 slices of fresh white
bread, crusts removed
and crumbled
4 Tbsp (1/2 stick) sweet
butter
4 Tbsp corn or peanut oil
2 lemons, cut in wedges

SERVES 4

Whisk the egg briskly in a large bowl.

Add mayonnaise, mustard, Worcestershire, Old Bay
seasoning, salt, and pepper. Continue whisking mixture
until smooth and creamy.

Add crabmeat, parsley, and finely crumbled soda
crackers.

Toss all ingredients lightly but well to mix thoroughly.

Divide the crab meat mixture into 8 portions, and
shape into small round patties about 1/2 inch thick.

Wrap patties in wax paper and refrigerate for 1 hour.

Heat butter and oil in a large heavy skillet until just
sizzling.

Fry crab cakes, turning once, until golden brown and
crispy on both sides.

Drain on paper towels and serve immediately with
lemon wedges on the side.

SERVES 4

Preheat oven to 450 F.

Thoroughly blend in onion, Worcestershire and bread cubes. Remove mixture from heat and let cool.

Thoroughly combine the crabmeat withall ingredients and pour into a buttered 1-qt casserole.

Sprinkle paprika on top, and bake for about 10 or 15 minutes until lightly browned and bubbling.

Ingredients

1 Tbsp Dijon mustard
generous pinch Old Bay
    seasoning
2 Tbsp Basic Mayonnaise
    (p. 23)
1/2 small onion, minced
dash Tobasco
1 tsp Worcestershire sauce
1/2 tsp lemon juice
sprinkling of freshly
    ground white pepper
1 lb fresh crabmeat,
    preferably backfin
paprika
1 small green pepper,
    diced
1 small red pepper, diced

BROILED
SOFT-SHELL CRABS

Ingredients

12 cleaned soft-shell crabs
4 oz (1/4 cup) bread
   crumbs
2 oz (4 Tbsp) olive oil

SERVES 4

Preheat broiler. Grease the broiling rack.

Pat crabs dry. Lightly coat with olive oil and sprinkle with bread crumbs.

Place soft shell crabs on the rack. Broil under high flame for 2 minutes per side.

Carefully place 3 crabs on each platter.

Serve at once, perhaps with french-fried potatoes and freshly sliced fresh tomatoes.

CRABMEAT QUICHE

SERVES 4-6

TO MAKE THE TART CRUST
Throughly mix flour, butter and shortening in a large bowl. Combine all other ingredients with flour mixture, kneading dough lightly into a smooth ball. Wrap in wax paper and refrigerate for 2 hours.

Preheat oven to 400 F. Roll out dough to fit a 10-inch fluted tart pan.

Prick the bottom of the pastry with a fork, and line the bottom with buttered foil, weighted with dried beans. Bake the pastry for 8 minutes until it has set. Remove foil and beans and return pastry to oven until lightly browned (about 2-3 minutes).

TO MAKE THE FILLING
Sauté shallots and red pepper in butter in a covered pan until soft (2–3 minutes). Add crabmeat and stir for 2 minutes. Add Sherry or Madeira, turn up heat for 2 minutes. Turn off heat and allow sauté mixture to cool.

In a mixing, bowl beat the eggs, cream, paprika, Worchestershire, salt and pepper. Blend in crabmeat mixture. Check seasoning.

Pour into pastry shell and sprinkle with cheese and paprika. Bake in top third of oven for 25–30 minutes until lighly brown.

Ingredients

TART CRUST
2 cups all-purpose flour
8 Tbsp (1 stick) cold butter, cut in 1/4-inch slices
5 Tbsp shortening, chilled
3/4 tsp salt
1/2 Tbsp butter for the foil
3 Tbsp chives, chopped
5 Tbsp ice water
1 Tbsp fresh lemon juice
FILLING
2 Tbsp minced shallots
1 red pepper, sliced thin
3 Tbsp butter
6 oz fresh crabmeat
2 Tbsp Sherry or Madeira
3 eggs
1 cup heavy cream
1 tsp Worchesershire sauce
1/4 tsp salt
sprinkling of black pepper
1/4 cup Swiss cheese, grated
1/2 tsp paprika

SOFT-SHELL CRABS
Pan-fried
with Rémoulade Sauce

Ingredients

12 medium soft-shell crabs
 (cleaned)
I cup all- purpose flour
2 oz clarified butter
i cup seasoned bread
 crumbs
rémoulade sauce (see p.
 31)

SERVES 4

Dust crabs with flour. Shake off excess.

Whisk eggs.

 Dip crabs in egg and dip in the bread crumbs. Shake off excess

Heat butter in a large skillet until sizzling. First fry the crabs belly side down for about 2 minutes. Turn and continue to fry for another 2 minutes or until nicely browned.

Remove crabs with tongs or slotted spoon. Drain on paper towels.

Serve immediately with rémoulade sauce.

SAUTÉED ABALONE
on
Fresh Leaf Spinach

SERVES 4

Briefly (about 45 seconds) sauté spinach in 1 Oz of melted butter, until spinach is just wilted.

Set aside in warm place.

Dredge each slice of abalone in flour. Shake off the excess.

Dip into beaten eggs.

Heat remaining 3 oz of butter in large skillet and sauté abalone over high heat, about 30 seconds on each side.

On a warm plate, place sautéed abalone on a bed of the cooked spinach

Ingredients

8 thin slices of abalone
1 lb carefully cleaned leaf
    spinach
1 cup flour
3 eggs, beaten
4 oz clarified butter
salt and pepper to taste

LOBSTER

A famous French gourmet once remarked that "a truly destitute man is not one without riches, but the poor wretch who has never partaken of a lobster." The awkward-looking creature with the two big claws, one larger than the other, is our North American and much-honored lobster that's taken in waters from Maine to the Carolinas.

For many seafood lovers even the word lobster conjures up the tangy smell of salt air, a bib tied around the neck, fingers ready, and an always unforgettable experience in fine eating. The spiny or rock lobster, sometimes called crayfish (and Florida lobster in the East), is caught in southern waters and shipped throughout the United States from Florida and California. The rock lobster has no claws, and since the meat is in the tail and easily removed, eating the southern lobster requires less work than its northern counterpart. For many people, that "work" is half the fun and pleasure in eating a lobster, so north or south it's just a matter of preference. To paraphrase Will Rogers: You'll never meet a lobster you won't like, as long as it was lively and fresh before it was cooked.

Lobsters mature slowly, and take approximately 6 years to reach a legal marketable weight of about 1 pound. The female lobster is supposedly tastier than the male, but the difference is so slight that only the most demanding expert would notice. The meat of the male lobster does seem to stay a bit firmer than the female when cooked, and again this is a matter of preference. The soft and smooth fin-like appendages on the underside of the female lobster where the body meets the tail distinguish the female from the male. The male lobster's appendages are bonier.

When buying lobsters, you should allow a 1 1/4 to 1 1/2–2 pound lobster for each person. Lobsters weighing over 3 pounds are ideal for many dishes such as salads (see p. 306), Lobster Newburg (p. 109), etc. A 2 1/2pound lobster will yield approximately 2 cups or 1 pound lobster meat, with the largest pieces of the succulent white meat in the tail and claws. It's a myth that jumbo lobsters 5 pounds and up are tough and chewy. The fact is that the average kitchen's pots won't accommodate a 10- or 20 pound lobster, and most amateur chefs are reluctant to wrestle with a monster of that size. If you've got the strength and the time and a kettle large enough, there's no reason you can't go out and buy the largest lobster you can find—or better still, order one. It will be just as good as the smaller version.

When you buy a fresh live lobster, the tail should curl up under the body when the lobster is picked up, and its eyes, legs, and every movable part should be active. Boiling is the easiest and most popular method of preparing lobster, and the first step in creating all lobster dishes except Broiled Live Lobster (see p. 111).

TO BOIL AND CLEAN LOBSTER

In a large heavy pot or kettle pour enough water to cover the lobster(s) you plan to cook. Measure the water by quarts, and add 1 Tbsp salt for each quart of water in the pot. Use seawater instead, if it's available. Bring the water to a good rolling boil.

Keep an eye on those sharp claws, and grab the lobster firmly from behind the head. Plunge it quickly into the boiling water. Let the water return to a second boil and reduce heat immediately.

Simmer lobster for 7 minutes for the first pound and 3 more minutes for each additional pound. When lobster is cooked, remove it from the water with tongs and let cool at room temperature. Its color will be bright red. If your lobster was alive and fresh when cooked, the tail will be firmly curled up under the body, and when straightened out it will spring back into place.

Place lobster on a counter top or board on its underside. With a sharp knife or scissors split the lobster down the back from head to tail. Remove the intestinal vein running from head to tail and the small sac behind the head.

Don't discard the green tomalley (liver), or the coral roe you may find in a female lobster. Both are delicious to eat with the lobster or added to the sauce for other dishes such as Lobster Newburg (see p. 109).

Crack claws with a nutcracker. The lobster is ready to eat, served with bowls of hot melted butter on the side. The lobster meat may be pried loose and removed from the shell with a small fork and a nut pick if it's to be used in other dishes.

BUTTER-FRIED LOBSTER

Ingredients

8 Tbsp (1 stick) sweet
  butter
1 1/4–1 1/2 lb cooked
  lobster meat, cut in
  large cubes
2 Tbsp dry Sherry
pinch of salt
8 sprigs of fresh parsley

SERVES 2-3

Melt butter in a large, heavy skillet over medium heat until hot but not sizzling.

Add lobster meat.

Lower heat and cover the skillet for about 3 minutes, until lobster meat heats through.

Remove the cover from the skillet and turn up the heat. Add Sherry and salt.

Sizzle lobster for about 2 or3 minutes, turning with tongs, until nicely browned on all sides.

Remove lobster to preheated serving plates with tongs or a slotted spoon.

Garnish with parsley sprigs.

LOBSTER CRÊPES
with Sea Scallops, Chanterelles, and Two Sauces

SERVES 4

Prepare the crêpes. Keep in a warm place.

Prepare the mousseline sauce. Set aside.

Sauté scallops in a skillet with the white wine for about 5 minutes. Drain scallops in a colander and reserve the liquid. Set the scallops aside in a warm place.

Cut the lobster meat into bite-size chunks. Melt the butter in a large heavy skillet and slowly stir in flour over low heat until thickened. Slowly blend in cream. Add the reserved liquid from the scallops and the Port wine.

Continue cooking, stirring over low heat until the mixture is creamy and smooth.

Add the lobster meat, scallops, and chanterelles. Season to taste with salt and pepper. Set the mixture aside in a warm place.

Preheat broiler. Roll crêpes (2 per serving) after spooning the filling onto crêpe. Set two rolled crêpes onto ovenproof serving plate and cover with some sauce from the mixture. Top with mousseline sauce.

Place under hot broiler for a few seconds until lightly browned on top. Serve at once.

Ingredients

crêpes (see p. 66)
mousseline sauce
    (see p. 27)
1/2 lb sea scallops
1/2 cup dry white wine
1/2 lb cooked lobster mea
4 Tbsp butter
4 Tbsp all-purpose flour
1 cup heavy cream
1/2 cup Port wine
1/2 lb fresh chanterelles
salt and pepper to taste

LOBSTER FLAMBÉ

Ingredients

8 Tbsp (1 stick) butter
2 Tbsp fresh chives,
    chopped
1 tsp curry powder
1 cup heavy cream
salt to taste
1 lb cooked lobster meat,
    cut in bite-size pieces
2 lobster claws, picked
    clean
3 oz Brandy

SERVES 4

Melt 4 Tbsp of the butter in a small heavy skillet.

Add chives and cook for about 1 minute.

Add the curry powder and stir well over low heat.

Gradually stir in cream and continue cooking over low heat until hot but not bubbling. Season with salt to taste. Keep hot over very low heat.

Meanwhile, melt remaining 4 Tbsp butter in a separate medium size heavy skillet.

Add lobster meat and heat well and evenly, stirring constantly for about 4 or 5 minutes.

When lobster is hot, pour Brandy over it.

Remove from heat and quickly set lobster meat ablaze with a match. Let blaze for about 30 seconds.

Arrange lobster meat on a preheated serving dish (or individual serving dishes) and pour hot cream sauce over all.

Garnish with lobster claws attractively arranged.

LOBSTER NEWBURG

SERVES 3-4

Melt butter in the top part of a double boiler.

Stir in lobster meat and cook over boiling water for about 3 minutes.

Add the Sherry or Madeira and continue cooking and stirring for 2 minutes.

Whisk cream and egg yolks together. Add the cream and yolks to the lobster.

Stir until smooth and the Newburg sauce begins to thicken.

Don't let the mixture boil and don't let the top part of the double boiler sit in the water.

Season with salt to taste.

Serve the Newburg on toast points or rice, and sprinkle with paprika before serving.

NOTE
Make a paste of the liver and the roe and blend it with the lobster meat for extra richness.

Ingredients

4 Tbsp (1/2 stick) sweet butter
1 lb cooked lobster meat, cut in bite-size pieces
1/4 cup dry Dry Sack
1 cup heavy cream
3 egg yolks
salt to taste
paprika

LOBSTER THERMIDOR

Ingredients

4 1 1/4 to 1 1/2 lb fresh
    live lobster
2 Tbsp butter
3 Tbsp flour
1 cup heavy cream
1 Tbsp Dijon mustard
1 cup Madeira or dry
    Sherry
1 cup dry white wine
salt and pepper
1 lb fresh, medium-size
    mushrooms, washed
    and quartered
mousseline sauce
    (see p. 27)

SERVES 4

Steam lobster for about 8 minutes. Set aside and cool.

Melt butter in a large, heavy skillet, and slowly stir in flour over low heat until thickened. Add heavy cream, dry Sherry or Madeira, and white wine, and Dijon mustard.

Continue stirring, always over low heat, until mixture is creamy and smooth. Add salt and pepper to taste. Set aside in warm place.

Split lobster in half. Remove meat from tail and claws. Cut lobster meat into bite-size pieces. Under warm water, clean shell, discarding any remains. Set the cleaned shells aside, ready to be filled.

Cut mushrooms into quarters. Sauté in butter. Add both lobster and mushrooms to the wine mixture. Reheat over low heat for 2 minute.

Preheat the broiler.

Place halved shells (shell side down) on a baking sheet. Fill with the mixture. Top with mousseline sauce (see p. 27). Put under the broiler until golden brown.

With a spatula, place two halves per serving onto warm serving plates. Serve with plain, steamed rice.

BROILED LIVE LOBSTER

SERVES 4

NOTE
Have your fish market split and clean the lobsters
unless you really know how to do it properly. It's not an
easy job.

Preheat broiler for about 10 minutes.

Thoroughly coat each lobster half with canola oil and
place on the broiler rack.

Sprinkle with bread crumbs

Broil with the shell side up 3 or 4 in from the flame for
about 7 or 8 minutes.

Turn the lobsters carefully with tongs.

Broil with the shell side down for about 7 or 8 minutes.

Baste lobsters with melted butter before serving.

Serve lobsters immediately with bowls of melted butter
and lemon wedges.

Ingredients

4 1 1/2 to 2 lb lobsters,
    split and cleaned
corn oil
1lb (4 sticks) sweet butter,
    melted
lemon wedges
seasoned bread crumbs

BROILED
LIVE STUFFED LOBSTER

Ingredients

1/4 cup fine bread
    crumbs
liver (tomalley) and if the
    lobsters are female, roe
    (coral)
1 Tbsp fresh lemon juice
    (or 1 Tbsp dry Sherry)
broiled, live lobster

INDIVIDUAL SERVING

Thoroughly blend all ingredients in a small bowl.

Spoon the stuffing mixture into the cavity of each
lobster.

Proceed as for BROILED LIVE LOBSTER (see p. 111),
except don't turn the lobsters.

Broil with the shell side down for about 15 or 16
minutes, basting frequently, or until done.

COLD LOBSTER
with Shallot-Tarragon-Curry Dressing

SERVES 4

In a large pot, steam the lobsters 7 minutes per pound. Chill.

When lobsters cool enough to handle, clean each. Remove the meat from the tails, break the claws open and remove each piece intact.

Save the legs from each. Keep the meat from each lobster separate from the others so that when plating the salad, each serving will consist of a whole lobster.

TO MAKE THE DRESSING
In a metal bowl, combine the egg yolks, shallots, curry, salt, pepper, and vinegar. Slowly whisk in the oil until ingredients are combined and the dressing thickens.

Mix in the chopped fresh tarragon. Wash the salad greens and spin them dry. Chop and mix them together. Toss with some of the dressing.

When ready to serve, put a bed of the lettuces in the middle of each plate. Arrange the claw meat and legs around the salad to look like a lobster.

Slice the tail meat and place it on top of the bed of mixed greens. Pour remaining dressing over tail portion and serve immediately.

Ingredients

4 1 lb lobsters
2 heads of frisée
4 bunches mache
2 heads of radicchio

FOR THE DRESSING

3 egg yolks
1 medium shallot, finely chopped
1 tsp curry powder
1/3 cup tarragon vinegar
salt and pepper to taste
1 cup vegetable oil
2 oz fresh tarragon, finely chopped

LOBSTER PIE

Ingredients

12 Tbsp (1 1/2 sticks)
    sweet butter, melted
1/2 cup Sherry
2 cups bite-size cooked
    lobster meat
2 Tbsp all-purpose flour
1 1/2 tsp salt
1 1/2 cups light cream
4 egg yolks
1/2 cup cracker meal
1 tsp paprika
1/4 cup crushed saltines
2 Tbsp Parmasean cheese,
    grated

INDIVIDUAL SERVING

Preheat oven to 300 F.

Boil 6 Tbsp of the melted butter with the Sherry in a medium-sized heavy saucepan for 2 minutes.

Remove from heat and add lobster to the Sherry butter.

Put 6 more Tbsp melted butter in the top part of a double boiler over hot but not boiling water.

Stir in flour and salt and add the cream and Sherry butter drained from the lobster.

Cook, stirring constantly, until the sauce begins to thicken. Remove from heat.

Beat egg yolks in a large bowl until thick. Gradually blend cream sauce into the yolks.

Return the sauce to the top of the double boiler and continue cooking over the simmering water for 3 minutes, stirring constantly. Add bite-size lobster and mix well.

Spoon lobster and sauce into 4 individual casseroles or baking dishes. Mix cracker meal, paprika, saltines (or potato chips), Parmesan cheese, and remaining melted butter. Sprinkle over the top of each dish.

MUSSELS

Mussels are more popular in Europe than in the United States, and although we have a plentiful supply of them clinging to the rocks of our shores on both coasts, the poor mussel remains our most neglected shellfish. This is unfortunate because they have a rich and delicious flavor, and Moules Mariniére (Steamed Mussels in White Wine, see p. 121), for instance, compares favorably with the finest of seafood dishes. Mussels are sold alive and in the shell, which is thin and blue-black and measures from 2 to 2 1/2 inches long. They're also available in cans. You can buy mussels in your fish market by the quart or by the dozen. Two quarts of mussels, or 4 dozen, are usually sufficient for 2 persons. Mussels are distinguished by a mass of vegetation on their shells, called a beard, which must be removed before steaming. They also have a tendency to be sandy, so they must be washed very well.

TO CLEAN MUSSELS

Scrub mussels thoroughly with a stiff brush under cold running water.
Snip off the beard from each mussel with a small pair of sharp scissors, or pul offl by a back and forth motion. Remove the beard before washing mussels.

Place mussels in a large kettle and cover with cold water.

Let the mussels stand for 2 hours, and immediately discard any that float.

TO COOK MUSSELS

Mussels must be steamed open for use in any dish.

Place mussels with 1 cup water in a large heavy saucepan or kettle. Add 1 tsp salt and cover the saucepan/kettle.

Steam over low heat for about 3 minutes, or just until the mussels open.

Remove mussels from the saucepan/kettle with a slotted spoon. Take the meat from the shells.

Snip off the beard from each mussel with a small pair of sharp scissors (if you haven't removed it before steaming).

Mussels are ready to prepare for your recipe.

MUSSEL FRITTERS

Ingredients

1 1/4 cups all-purpose
flour
1/4 tsp salt
2 tsp baking powder
1 egg
2/3 cup half-and-half
1/4 cup broth from the
steamed mussels
(reserve the rest of the
broth for later use)
4 dozen mussels, bearded,
steamed open, removed
from shells, and
coarsely chopped
pinch of salt
sprinkling of ground white
pepper
pinch of paprika
peanut oil for deep frying

SERVES 4-6

Combine flour, salt, baking powder, egg, half-and-half, and broth from the steamed mussels in a large bowl.

Beat thoroughly until well blended.

Season mussels with salt, pepper, and paprika, and fold into the batter.

Heat oil for deep frying to 375 F in a large heavy kettle or Dutch oven. A piece of bread dropped into the oil will turn golden brown when the temperature of the oil is just right.

Drop tablespoonfuls of the batter into the oil and fry until golden brown, about 3 to 5 minutes.

Drain fritters on paper towels.

MUSSELS AU GRATIN

SERVES 4-6

Preheat oven to 350 F.

Melt 4 Tbsp of the butter in a large heavy skillet.

Add onion and sauté for about 5 minutes or until golden. Slowly add flour, stirring constantly over low heat.

When flour is well blended, gradually add broth from the steamed mussels.

Continue stirring over low heat until the sauce begins to thicken. Add salt, pepper, and Sherry, and continue stirring.

In a casserole or baking dish arrange alternate layers of mussels, sauce, cracker crumbs, and a light sprinkling of cheese until all ingredients have been used.

Crumble crackers between waxed paper with a rolling pin for fine crumbs, or coarse if you prefer them.

Reserve just enough crumbs and cheese to sprinkle over the top of the casserole. Dot the top with the remaining 4 Tbsp butter.

Bake for about 15 minutes or until the top is golden brown.

Ingredients

8 Tbsp (1 stick) sweet butter
1 small onion, minced
4 Tbsp all-purpose flour
1 cup broth from the steamed mussels
1/2 tsp salt
sprinkling of ground white pepper
1/4 cup Sherry
4 dozen mussels, bearded, steamed open, and removed from shells
1 cup crackers, finely crumbled
1/2 cup Cheddar cheese, finely crumbled

BAKED MUSSELS
in White Wine

Ingredients

4 dozen mussels, bearded,
    steamed open, and
    removed from shells
1 tsp salt
ground white pepper
pinch of paprika
1 tsp fresh dill, finely
    chopped (or dried dill
    may be used instead)
1 small onion, minced
1/2 cup dry white wine
1 Tbsp Parmesan cheese,
    grated
4 slices very lean bacon,
    cubed

SERVES 4-6

Preheat oven to 350 F.

Place mussels in a shallow casserole or baking dish.

Season them with salt, pepper, paprika, and dill.

Sprinkle onion over all and pour in the wine.

Top with Parmesan cheese.

Arrange bacon slices on top of cheese.

Bake for about 15 minutes or until the bacon is crisp.

MOULES MARINIÉRE
(Mussels Steamed
in White Wine)

SERVES 4-6

Put onion, garlic, and parsley in a large heavy kettle or saucepan.

Add mussels and sprinkle generously with pepper.

Put in 4 Tbsp butter and pour the wine over all.

Cover the kettle/saucepan and steam the mussels over low heat just until they open.

If any of the mussels don't open, discard them immediately.

Remove the mussels with a slotted spoon and place them in individual soup bowls.

Add 3 Tbsp butter to the broth, stir, and bring just to a boil. Pour the broth over the mussels before serving.

Serve the French bread on the side for dipping.

Ingredients

1 small onion, minced
3 garlic cloves, minced
1 Tbsp fresh parsley, minced
4 dozen mussels, bearded, and in their shells
generous sprinkling of ground black pepper
7 Tbsp sweet butter
1 cup dry white wine
large loaf of crusty French bread, split lengthwise and quartered (but not sliced all the way through)

BAKED STUFFED MUSSELS

Ingredients

2 dozen mussels, bearded,
    steamed open,
        removed from shells,
        and coarsely chopped.
        Reserve half shells
1 clove garlic, minced
1 small onion, minced
5 Tbsp sweet butter
1 cup fresh spinach,
    cooked, drained, and
    finely chopped pPinch
    of salt
sprinkling of ground black
    pepper
1/4 cup fine bread
    crumbs
1/4 cup Parmesan cheese,
    grated
1/2 tsp paprika

SERVES 4-6

Preheat oven to 450 F.

Arrange mussel half shells on a baking sheet (or the mussels may be baked on rock salt (see Baked Stuffed clams, p. 92).

Sauté garlic and onion and 3 Tbsp butter in a large heavy skillet until onion is golden.

Lightly blend mussels and all other ingredients except remaining 2 Tbsp butter.

Spoon the mixture into the half shells.

Dot with butter and bake until lightly browned on top.

BLACK SEA MUSSELS
in Raspberry Vinaigrette

SERVES 6-8

Marinate mussels in raspberry vinaigrette for 1 hour.

Add red pepper and leeks and serve over bed of mixed greens.

TO MAKE VINAIGRETTE

Mix raspberry vinegar, olive oil, salt and pepper to taste.

Ingredients

5 dozen mussels, steamed
and taken out of shell
1/2 cup raspberry vinegar
1 cup olive oil
1/4 tsp salt
1 red pepper, chopped
1 leek, julienned
1 lb mixed greens

OYSTERS

The joy of eating oysters has been celebrated by seafood lovers the world over, almost since time began. The Britons had plentiful oyster beds as early as 55 B.C. When the Romans invaded Britain, they became so captivated by the exquisite flavor of the oyster that they began shipping them back to Rome in bags of snow and ice. No true Roman banquet was ever complete if the menu did not include chilled raw oysters on the half shell, and a real gourmand could dispense with 5 or 6 dozen before going onto the next course.

The French were so enamored of oysters that in the mid-1800s it was necessary to call in the navy to guard a rapidly diminishing supply of France's tasty mollusks. Giovanni Giacomo,the dashing Venetian rascal also known as Casanova, attributed at least part of his reputation as a great lover to the dozens of oysters he consumed every day. The Greeks, Danes, Irish, and American Indians, among others, all feasted on oysters many centuries ago, with each group preparing and serving them raw or roasted, plain or seasoned, according to custom and individual taste.

Oysters today are as much appreciated for their nutritive value as for their epicurean qualities, and they have never enjoyed wider popularity. In Ireland every year Galway sets aside the second week of September to toast the oyster with three days of banquets, parades, dancing, and an international oyster-shucking contest that attracts contestants from ten countries including the United States.

On the Delmarva Peninsula, which encompasses Delaware, Maryland, and Virginia, in New Orleans, New England, and the state of Washington, and on Prince Edward Island in Canada and the West Coast of France in Brittany, the oyster is honored throughout the year.

And of course the celebration of the oyster never ends at The Oyster Bar, where between 15and 30 varieties from different areas are served daily year round, depending on the quality available. Cotuit and Wellfleet oysters are trucked down several times a week from

Cotuit Harbor on Nantucket Sound and Wellfleet Harbor in Cape Cod, Massachusetts; Chincoteague, Kent Island, oysters come up from the South. The Belon comes in from Blue Hill, Maine. Whenever Canadian Malpeque oysters are available, they're shipped from Prince Edward Island, in an often complicated route by which they arrive at The Oyster Bar fresh. Sometimes the Malpeques are put aboard the first tuna boat that's leaving Port, or they may "hitchhike" and share a chartered plane with other express foods coming into New York. If The Oyster Bar's daily shipment of lobsters is leaving when the Canadian oysters arrive in Maine, they'll be brought in on the same truck. However they arrive, most people agree they're worth any difficulty in getting them here. The popular bluepoints and the larger box oysters come in from Long Island. At certain times of the year the tiny Olympia oysters from Puget Sound are flown in and rushed to the restaurant from the airport. In addition, The Oyster Bar cultivates its own oyster beds in Westport, Connecticut.

You'll notice that many seafood stores still display "Oysters R in Season" signs, which traditionally meant that oysters were available only during months that have the letter R, with the season beginning in September. The slogan is clever, but it doesn't have any meaning, since oysters may be eaten all year round. Oysters reproduce from May through August, and though in some instances they may not be quite as plump and tasty as during the R months, it's certainly safe to eat them year round as long as they've been properly refrigerated.

Raw oysters are best served ice cold on the half shell in a bed of ice, with Cocktail Sauce or Shallot Sauce (see pp. 9 and 36). They're also superb in the famous Oyster Stew (see p. 58) or Oyster Pan Roast (see p. 62) and in crisp and tasty Oyster Fritters Maryland (see p.131). You'll buy oysters by the dozen in their shells, or already shucked and in their own liquor by the pint and quart. If the oysters have been freshly opened by your fish store, you must use them immediately. Oysters have a shallow shell on one side and a deep shell on the other. It's in the deep shell that they're usually served. If you're going to be doing your own shucking, you'll have to invest in an inexpensive but absolutely necessary oyster knife. Opening oysters takes a bit of practice, but once you learn how to do it the process becomes quite simple. Oysters should be well iced or chilled in their shells and opened just before you plan to serve them. Six oysters on the half shell are usually served for one person, although some people can handle a dozen comfortably if your main course is light. Instead of serving a sauce, you may prefer to sprinkle each oyster with a few drops of fresh lemon juice and ground black pepper. After the oyster is eaten, its tasty liquor should be sipped right from the shell.

TO SHUCK OYSTERS

Scrub oysters thoroughly with a stiff brush under cold running water.

Discard any oysters with broken or gaping shells.

Hold the oyster flat on a table or counter top with your left hand, with the thin end of the oyster pointed toward you. Cover top of oyster with a towel to protect your hand.

With your right hand, force the oyster knife between the shells at the thin end. If you have difficulty doing this, break off a bit of the thin end with a hammer so the knife can be inserted more easily.

NOTE
One problem with this practice is that bits of the shell may get into the oyster, making it gritty.

Try to avoid plunging the knife straight into the oyster, but rather keep the knife against the shell.

Move the knife sharply left and right to cut the oyster's large abductor muscle attached to the shell.

Remove the shell with a twisting motion.

Cut the other end of the same muscle attached to the opposite shell.

Remove any bits of broken shell from the oyster before serving.

OYSTER PUFFS

Ingredients

1 dozen oysters, shucked
   and with liquor
1/2 cup half-and-half
2 Tbsp (1/4 stick) butter
2 tsp salt
1/2 tsp sugar
1 cup all-purpose flour
4 eggs
Peanut oil for deep frying

SERVES 3-4

In a large, heavy saucepan simmer oysters in their liquor until the edges begin to curl. Remove oysters from the liquor with a slotted spoon and pat dry on a paper towel. Chop the oysters fine.

Bring oyster liquor, half-and-half, butter, salt, and sugar to a boil in the saucepan.

Add flour all at once. Stir mixture constantly over low heat until batter forms a smooth consistency. There should be no flour sticking to the sides of the saucepan. Remove batter from heat.

Cool for a few minutes before adding eggs, one at a time. Beat mixture thoroughly after each egg is added. Blend in chopped oysters and mix well.

Heat oil for deep frying to 375 F in a large, heavy kettle or Dutch oven.

Drop tablespoonsful of the batter into the oil and fry until golden brown, about 3 to 5 minutes. Drain on paper towels.

Puffs go well with cocktail sauce (see p. 9) or Tartar sauce (see p. 39).

BROILED OYSTERS
with Anchovy Butter

SERVES 2

Preheat the broiler for about 10 minutes.

Place oysters in a single layer on a baking sheet.

Put 1 slice of anchovy butter on top of each oyster.

Broil for about 1 or 2 minutes until lightly browned.

Place oyster on plate, and top with anchovy butter from pan.

Garnish with chopped parsley.

Ingredients

1 dozen oysters, shucked
and drained (reserve
oyster liquor and set
aside for another use),
on the half shell
anchovy butter (see p. 4)
4 sprigs chopped parsley

POACHED
WELLFLEET OYSTERS
over Shiitake Mushrooms
Beurre Blanc

Ingredients

18 Wellfleet oysters,
   shucked, with liquid
   reserved
18 medium size Shiitake
   mushrooms
2 cloves garlic
4 sprigs freshly washed
   parsley
1 cup white wine
1 Tbsp butter
salt and pepper to taste
1 pt *beurre blanc*
   (see p.7)

SERVES 3-4

Separate the stems from the cap of the mushrooms. Set caps aside. Dice stems, garlic and parsley.

Sauté mushroom mixture in butter for about 5 minutes.

Add wine and reduce until dry.

Set aside in a warm place.

Slice off top of each mushroom cap so it will stand on serving plate. Grill mushroom caps and set aside in warm place.

Proceed to make *beurre blanc*.

When the *beurre blanc* is ready, proceed to poach the oysters in their own liquid (any oyster or clam juice can be used as a substitute or augmentation) until they are curled at the edges.

Place mushroom caps on a small serving plate and top with mixture of mushroom, garlic and parsley. Place <u>hot</u> oyster on top. Pour a small amount of *beurre blanc* on each cap.

NOTE
Beurre blanc should be a little runny.

OYSTER FRITTERS MARYLAND

SERVES 4

Drain oysters, and set liquor aside for later use if necessary.

Thoroughly mix milk, pancake mix, cornmeal, salt, and pepper in a large bowl.

Gently fold oysters into the batter.

Heat oil and butter in a 10-inch skillet until just sizzling.

Drop batter into the skillet by the tablespoonful.

Be sure that two oysters are included with each tablespoonful.

Fry until golden brown on one side, about 2 minutes.

Turn each fritter carefully with tongs and brown on the other side for about 2 minutes.

If batter becomes too thick while standing, thin it with a few drops of oyster liquor.

Reserve the remaining oyster liquor for another use.

Drain fritters on a paper towel. Serve with lemon wedges or any favorite seafood sauce.

Ingredients

30 oysters, shucked and with liquor
1/2 cup evaporated milk
1 cup dry pancake mix
2 Tbsp cornmeal
1 tsp salt
Generous sprinkling of ground black pepper
1 cup corn oil
2 Tbsp (1/4 stick) sweet butter

OYSTERS CASINO

Ingredients

3 slices bacon, coarsely
    chopped
1 small onion, finely
    chopped
1 small red pepper, finely
    chopped
2 Tbsp white wine
1 small green pepper,
    finely chopped
1 small stalk celery, finely
    chopped
1 tsp lemon juice
1 tsp salt
generous sprinkling of
    ground black pepper
generous dash of
    Worcestershire sauce
3 or 4 drops Tabasco
    sauce
1/4 tsp seafood seasoning
1 dozen oysters, shucked
    and drained (reserve
    oyster liquor and set
    aside for another use)

SERVES 2

Preheat oven to 400 F.

Fry bacon in a large, heavy skillet until almost crisp.

Add onion, red and green pepper, celery, and all
seasonings, and white wine.

Sauté until vegetables are just tender.

Arrange oysters in a single layer in a large shallow
baking dish or casserole lined with foil.

Spread the bacon and vegetable mixture carefully over
the top of the oysters.

Bake for about 10 minutes or until the edges of the
oysters begin to curl.

Serve on hot toast points or a handful of oyster
crackers.

PANFRIED OYSTERS

SERVES 4

Drain oysters and pat dry.

Thoroughly mix flour and bread crumbs in a bowl.

Beat eggs with cream and salt and pepper in another bowl.

Roll oysters in crumb and flour mixture, then in egg, and then in crumbs again, coating thoroughly.

Heat butter in a large skillet over medium heat until just sizzling.

Fry oysters until nicely browned on one side, 3–5 minutes.

Turn carefully with tongs, and brown on the other side for 3–5 minutes.

Drain on paper towels.

Serve with lemon wedges or a favorite seafood sauce.

Ingredients

2 dozen oysters, shucked and drained (reserve liquor)
1 cup all-purpose flour
1 cup fine bread crumbs
2 eggs, beaten
2 Tbsp light cream
1 tsp salt
generous sprinkling of ground white pepper
8 Tbsp (1 stick) sweet butter

OYSTERS ROCKEFELLER

Ingredients

4 pie or cake tins, half
    filled with rock salt
2 dozen oysters, opened
    and on the half shell
4 medium shallots, minced
    (about 1/4 cup)
1 small stalk celery, minced
1 tsp fresh chervil, minced
    (or 1/2 tsp dried
    chervil may be used)
1/4 cup fresh parsley,
    minced
1/2 lb (2 sticks)
    sweet butter
2 cups fresh spinach,
    coarsely chopped
1/3 cup soft bread crumbs
1 or 2 drops
    Worcestershire sauce
1/2 tsp salt
sprinkling of ground black
    pepper
dash of Pernod or anisette

SERVES 4

Preheat oven to 450 F.

Place the tins with the rock salt in the oven.

Prepare the oysters.

Sauté shallots, celery, chervil, and parsley in 4 Tbsp (1/2 stick) of the butter in a heavy skillet.

Add spinach to the skillet and let it wilt for a minute.

Pour spinach mixture into an electric blender with the remaining butter, bread crumbs, seasonings, and Pernod or anisette.

Blend for 1 minute at medium speed.

Top each oyster with about 1 tablespoonful of this mixture.

Remove the tins from the oven and embed the oysters firmly in the hot salt.

Return pans to the oven and bake for about 4 minutes or until the butter is melted and oysters are lightly browned on top

Serve oysters right in the tin.

SCALLOPED OYSTERS

SERVES 6

Preheat oven to 350 F.

Drain oysters, and set liquor aside, measuring out 1/2 cup.

Reserve the remaining oyster liquor for another use.

Arrange alternate layers of oysters and crackers in a 2-qt, lightlybuttered casserole or baking dish.

Dot each layer with butter and season with salt and pepper.

End each layer with a topping of crackers.

Thoroughly mix half-and-half milk, and oyster liquor.

Pour into the casserole.

Sprinkle paprika on top and bake until nicely browned, about 50 to 60 minutes.

Ingredients

- 1 qt (approximately 60) oysters, shucked and with liquor
- 3 cups oyster crackers, coarsely crumbled (or saltines may be used instead)
- 8 Tbsp (1 stick) sweet butter)
- generous sprinkling of ground white pepper
- 1 tsp salt, or to taste
- 1 cup half-and-half
- 1/2 cup milk
- 1/2 cup oyster liquor
- 1 tsp paprika

BLANQUETTE DE BELONS
aux Poireaux with a Julienne of Leeks

Ingredients

18 Belon oysters on half shell
1 cup white wine cream sauce (see p. 33)
2 leeks, white part only, julienne
1 oz parsley, chopped

SERVES 3-4

Shuck Belons and remove oyster and juice.

Put into medium sauce pan and add leeks and white wine cream sauce.

Simmer uncovered for 3 minutes.

Put oysters back into shell with a slotted spoon and top with leeks and sauce.

Garnish with chopped parslely.

OYSTERS FRIED
in a Corn Meal Batter

SERVES 3-4

Drain and dry shucked oysters.

Place in flour and shake off excess.

Mix eggs and milk well.

Dip oysters in egg and milk mixture, then in mix of cornmeal and bread crumbs.

Deep fry at 375 F till golden brown.

Serve with Tartar sauce (see p. 39).

Ingredients

45 oysters, shucked
1/2 cup flour
4 eggs
1/4 cup milk
2 cups cornmeal
2 cups bread crumbs
salt and white pepper to
　taste
8 oz Tartar sauce (see p.
　39)

SCALLOPS

The scallop is named for its beautifully fluted, scalloped shell, and there are two types—bay and sea. The bay scallop is much smaller, sweeter, and more tender than its relative from the sea, although the firm meat of both bay and sea scallops can be equally delicious when prepared with a light and sure hand. The sea scallop measures about 1 1/2 inches long and 1 inch thick, and it's often cut in half or sliced for various dishes. Scallops are sold by the pound. Allow 1/3 to 1/2 pound for each serving, depending on the recipe.

Occasionally you'll find scallops sold in the shell, or you may be lucky enough to pick them up at the shore yourself. They may be steamed open, but to avoid losing any flavor and to prevent them from drying out, place them in a preheated 300 F oven with the deepest shell side down until they open. The scallop we eat is the muscle that controls the scallop's movement; this is easily removed (and trimmed) from the shell.

Fresh scallops have a distinctive sweet odor, which you'll instantly recognize once you remove a freshly taken scallop from its shell.

SCALLOP BROIL

Ingredients

2 lb bay or sea scallops
8 Tbsp (1 stick) sweet
    butter, melted
1 large garlic clove,
    minced or mashed
1 tsp salt
generous sprinkling of
    ground white pepper
pinch of cayenne
1/4 cup flour
1 tsp paprika
8 sprigs of fresh parsley
2 lemons, cut in small
    wedges

SERVES 4-6

Preheat broiler for about 10 minutes.

Pat scallops dry with a paper towel.

Melt the butter with garlic in a small heavy saucepan.

Swish half the garlic butter (4 Tbsp) around the sides and bottom of a shallow baking dish or casserole.

Arrange the scallops in a single layer in the baking dish/casserole.

Season with salt, pepper, and cayenne.

Thoroughly mix flour and paprika and dust the scallops with this mixture.

Pour the remaining garlic butter over all.

Slide the baking dish/casserole under the broiler for about 6 to 8 minutes, or until the scallops are golden brown.

Garnish with parsley sprigs and lemon wedges before serving.

PANFRIED LANGOUSTINES AND SEA SCALLOPS
with Calvados Beurre Blanc

SERVES 4-6

Make Calvados *beurre blanc* (see below). Set aside

Flour and pan fry scallops and *langoustines* for 4–5 minutes.

Add 1/4 cup Calvados and 1 Tbsp chives. Flame and cook on low heat for 1 minute.

Mix the rice and apple mixture with the béchamel sauce. Extra béchamel may be refrigerated.

On each plate place 3 *langoustines* and 3 scallops on a bed of the rice, apple, and béchamel mixture and top with 2 oz Calvados *beurre blanc* .

Serve hot.

TO MAKE CALVADOS *BEURRE BLANC*

Follow directions for *beurre blanc* (see p. 7) and add apples and 1 cup Calvados during the cooking process. Set aside.

Ingredients

- 12 large *langoustines*
- 12 large cleaned sea scallops
- 4 oz flour
- 1 1/4 cup Calvados
- 1 Tbsp chives, chopped
- 2 Granny Smith apples, sliced
- 1/2 cup cooked white rice
- 8 oz Calvados *beurre blanc* sauce
- 2 oz béchamel (see p. 5)

SCALLOPS IN BUTTER AND VERMOUTH
on Toast Points

Ingredients

1 1/2 lb bay scallops
6 Tbsp (3/4 stick)
    sweet butter
1/4 cup dry vermouth
4 slices hot toast
1 Tbsp fresh chives,
    minced

SERVES 4-6

Pat scallops dry with a paper towel.

Melt butter in a large, heavy skillet.

Add scallops and sauté for about 2 or 3 minutes, tossing them lightly until just opaque. Do not overcook.

Add vermouth and keep over low heat until warm.

Spoon scallops onto hot toast, sliced diagonally, and sprinkle with chives.

SCALLOPS PROVENÇALE

SERVES 4

Peel, seed, and dice the tomatoes and strain out the seeds.

Place the tomatoes and the tomato liquid in an covered saucepan and keep hot over a low flame.

In a medium-sized skillet kheat oil and butterover high heat.

Dip the scallops first into the wine, then coat them with flour.

Sauté scallops in the combined hot oil and butter until they are golden.

Season with salt and pepper, and remove to a platter.

Add the garlic, cook 1 minute.

Add the onion, cook 2 minutes.

Add the tomatoes, cook 5 minutes.

Put the scallops back in the pan and stir well.

Sprinkle with the minced parsley and serve hot.

Ingredients

6 medium tomatoes
24 large scallops
1/2 cup white wine
1 cup flour
3 Tbsp olive oil
4 Tbsp sweet butter
salt and pepper to taste
3 garlic c loves, crushed
1 onion, medium, diced
3 Tbsp lemon juice
4 parsley sprigs
3 Tbsp minced parsley
4 Tbsp fresh basil,
   chopped

SCALLOPS MEUNIÉRE

Ingredients

2 lb bay scallops
1/2 cup milk
1/2 cup all-purpose flour
1 tsp salt
sprinkling of ground white
   pepper
1/2 cup peanut oil
4 Tbsp (1/2 stick) sweet
   butter
2 Tbsp fresh lemon juice
2 Tbsp fresh parsley,
   minced

SEVES 6-8

Soak scallops in milk for 15 minutes.

Drain off milk and pat scallops dry on a paper towel.

Season the flour with salt and pepper.

Roll the scallops in the flour and coat thoroughly.

Heat the oil in a large, heavy skillet until hot but not sizzling.

Sauté scallops in the oil, tossing them lightly for about 3–4 minutes until golden brown on all sides. Do not overcook.

Remove scallops from the skillet and drain on a paper towel.

Set aside and keep warm in a heated serving dish.

Wipe remaining oil from the skillet with a paper towel, add butter and heat until just foamy.

Stir in lemon juice and parsley.

Pour the butter over the scallops and serve.

PANFRIED BAY SCALLOPS

SERVES 6-8

Dredge scallops in flour to coat.

Sauté in clarified butter until golden brown.

Pat dry with paper towel or shake in colander to remove excess liquid.

Salt and pepper to taste.

Serve immediately.

Ingredients

2 lb bay scallops
1 cup flour
4 oz clarified butter
salt
pepper

BAY SCALLOPS IN PORT CREAM SAUCE
with Julienne of Leeks

Ingredients

2 lb of bay scallops
1 cup flour
1 cup heavy cream
4 oz clarified butter
1/2 cup of dry white
    wine.
1 cup dry Port
4 leeks (julienne the white
    part only)
salt and pepper to taste

SERVES 6-8

Dredge scallops in flour. Shake off excess.

Sauté in clarified butter over high heat for 5 minutes. Remove, drain, and set aside.

In same pan, deglaze with white wine and Port. Add julienne of leeks.

Cook until half reduced.

Add heavy cream, continue to reduce, adding salt and pepper. When reduced to consistency of a medium thick sauce, add scallops. Do not overcook.

Spoon mixture onto warm serving plates, making sure to divide scallops into equal portions.

Spoon Port cream sauce over ingredients and serve.

BAY SCALLOPS
on an Artichoke Heart with Mousseline Sauce

SERVES 6-8

Cook artichokes in salted water until the bottom is soft to the touch. Add 1 cup white wine vinegar and salt to prevent discoloration.

With scissors, trim sharp needle part of upper leaves. Clean inside of artichokes and set aside in warm place under a wet towel.

Simmer the scallops in white wine for about 5 minute. Drain.

Add the white wine sauce.

Prepare the mousseline sauce.

Spoon mixture into hot artichokes.

Top with mousseline sauce. Place under broiler for a few minutes until golden brown.

Ingredients

4 medium artichokes
1 cup white wine vinegar
1 Tbsp salt
1/2 lemon
2 lb bay scallops
1 cup dry white wine
1/2 cup white wine sauce
  (p.32)
mousseline sauce (p. 27)
salt and pepper to taste

COQUILLES ST. JACQUES

Ingredients

1 lb bay scallops
1/2 cup dry white wine
mousseline sauce
    (p. 27)
white wine sauce (p. 32)

SERVES 3-4

Preheat broiler for about 10 minutes.

In a skillet, simmer scallops in white wine for about 5 minutes.

Drain and reserve the liquid. Keep the scallops in a warm place.

Make the mousseline sauce and prepare the white wine sauce.

Add the scallops to the white wine sauce. and mix.

Spoon thescallop mixture into large scallop shells or shell-shaped oven proof individual dishes.

Top with mousseline sauce and place under broiler for a few moments until sauce is lightly browned on top.

Serve immediately.

FRIED SCALLOPS

SERVES 4

Pat scallops dry with a paper towel.

Beat eggs with milk until foamy.

Season bread crumbs with salt and pepper.

Dip scallops first in flour, then in egg and then in bread crumbs, coating thoroughly.

Arrange scallops on a platter in a single layer and chill in the refrigerator for 1 hour.

When they're ready to cook, heat oil in a large, heavy skillet or Dutch oven to 375 F. A piece of bread dropped into the oil will turn golden when the temperature of the oil is just right.

Fry scallops for about 2 to 3 minutes until golden brown. Do not overcook.

Drain on paper towels.

Serve with Tartar sauce and wedges of lemon.

Ingredients

1 1/2 lb bay or sea scallops (if using sea scallops, cut them in half)
2 eggs, beaten
1 cup flour
3 Tbsp cold milk
1 cup fine bread crumbs
1 tsp salt
sprinkling of ground white pepper
canola oil for deep frying
Tartar sauce (see p.39)
2 lemons, cut in wedges

HONEY-CURRIED SCALLOPS

Ingredients

1 1/2–2 lb sea scallops
1/4 cup honey
2 tsp curry powder
1/2 cup Dijon mustard
2 tsp fresh lemon juice

SERVES 4-6

Preheat broiler for about 10 minutes.

Pat scallops dry with a paper towel.

Thoroughly blend honey, curry powder, mustard, and lemon juice in a bowl.

Arrange the scallops in a single layer in a lightly buttered shallow baking dish or casserole lined with foil.

Brush scallops generously with the honey-curry sauce.

Slide the baking dish/casserole under the broiler (in the lowest position under the heat) for 5 minutes.

Turn scallops gently and brush the other side with the honey-curry sauce. Broil for 5 minutes more.

Saffron rice is good with this dish, and a bed of fresh, cooked, and slightly crisp buttered greens (such as spinach, kale, collards, etc.) are also interesting accompaniments.

OVEN-TOASTED SCALLOPS

SERVES 4-6

Preheat oven to 450 F.

Pat scallops dry with a paper towel.

Beat eggs with milk until foamy.

Season cracker crumbs with salt, pepper, thyme, and dill.

Dip scallops first in egg and then in cracker crumbs, coating thoroughly.

Arrange the scallops in a single layer in a shallow casserole or baking dish.

Pour melted butter over all.

Bake the scallops for about 15 minutes.

Serve with Tartar sauce or any favorite seafood sauce on the side.

Ingredients

1 1/2 lb sea scallops
2 eggs, beaten
2 Tbsp milk
1 cup cracker crumbs, coarsely crumbled
1 tsp salt
sprinkling of ground white pepper
1/2 tsp thyme
14 tsp fresh dill, minced (or dillweed may be used instead)
4 Tbsp (1/2 stick) sweet butter, melted
Tartar sauce (see p. 39)

BROILED SEA SCALLOPS
with Fresh Tarragon

Ingredients

2 lb fresh sea scallops
2 Tbsp bread crumbs
2 oz fresh chopped
   tarragon
4 sprigs of fresh tarragon

SERVES 6-8

Preheat broiler.

Combine sea scallops, and chopped tarragon in a
bowl and mix well.

Arrange coated scallops on a broiler rack and broil for
3 minutes (about 6 inches from the flame). Turn once
and continue to broil for another 2 to 3 minutes.

Arrange on the plate, placing fresh tarragon leaves on
top.

Serve immediately.

BROILED SEA SCALLOPS
with Their Roe and
Tarragon Beurre Blanc

SERVES 6-8

In a small saucepan, prepare the *beurre blanc*, using fresh tarragon and tarragon vinegar.

Set aside and keep warm

Add 1 tsp of the chopped tarragon. Cook over medium heat, reducing the liquid by one-third.

Place reduction into the top part of a double boiler and incorporate the butter by whisking it in very gradually. Pass the sauce through a fine sieve.

Keep warm. Add the *beurre blanc* and stir.

Carefully coat the sea scallops with bread crumbs, trying not to separate or break them.

Arrange coated scallops on a rack and broil for 2–3 minutes, turn and broil for another minute.

On a warm plate, spoon tarragon *beurre blanc* to cover bottom. Sprinkle with chopped tarragon. Arrange hot sea scallops and garnish each plate with a sprig of fresh tarragon.

Serving suggestion: boiled potatoes and sautéed *haricots verts*.

Ingredients

beurre blanc (see p. 7)
2 tsp chopped tarragon
1 sprig freshtarragon
2 lb sea scallops with their
   roe intact
1/2 cup seasoned bread
   crumbs
1/4 cup fresh chopped
   tarragon
4 sprigs fresh tarragon
   leaves

STEAMED SEA SCALLOPS
on Seaweed with
Gorgeous Green Sauce

Ingredients

2 lb fresh sea scallops
fresh seaweed (about 2
    handfulls,5–7 oz)
beurre blanc (see p. 7)
1 Tbsp chopped parsley
1/4 cup parsley,cooked
    and chopped
fresh spinach leaf,
    puréed

SERVES 6-8

First, layer the bottom part of 4 Chinese-style bamboo steamers (about 5 or 6 inches diameter) with seaweed.

Place sea scallops on top of seaweed. Average amount per serving will be 6 to 8 large scallops.

Steam for 3 to 5 minutes.

When the scallops are no longer shiny, but begin to have a dull appearance, they are cooked.

Prepare *beurre blanc* sauce.When cooking *beurre blanc*, add chopped parsley and puréedspinach leaf to give a green color.

Serve immediately in the bamboo steamer, with the green sauce on the side.

SHRIMP
PRAWNS
SCAMPI

If a survey were taken it would undoubtedly prove that more shrimp are sold in the United States every year than any other shellfish. The popularity of shrimp cocktail, fried shrimp, and scampi, and the versatility that this shellfish brings to so many other dishes have made it a staple in American seafood cuisine. Shrimp are usually sold in the fish market without the heads and in their paper-thin shells. If you're preparing scampi or some other broiled/fried dish, be sure to have the tails left on. Sizes of shrimp range from small to jumbo, and how you plan to use the shrimp will determine the size you buy. One pound of shrimp divided between 2 persons is usually sufficient for most dishes. If the shrimp will be heavily sauced, breaded, or included in a recipe with other ingredients, it's possible to stretch a pound into 3 and sometimes even 4 servings. But don't skimp! Jumbo shrimp are particularly impressive and attractive for a shrimp cocktail.

Whatever size you purchase, the shrimp should have a good gray-greenish color and its flesh will be firm if it's fresh. Shrimp is usually cleaned after cooking except when used in certain dishes (see Note p. 157). Happily, the cleaning of shrimp, whether raw or cooked, is an easy job.

TO CLEAN RAW SHRIMP

Wash the shrimp thoroughly under cold water.

Slit the shrimp down the back with a sharp knife, and peel off the shell.

Carefully pick out the black vein of the back with the tip of your knife.

Shrimp is ready to be cooked.

TO COOK SHRIMP

Drop shrimp into rapidly boiling water in a large heavy saucepan. Add 1 Tbsp salt for every quart of water in the saucepan.

Be sure the shrimp are completely covered with water.

When water reaches boiling point again, reduce heat.

Simmer shrimp for 1 to 3 minutes until just pink and tender. Don't overcook.Smaller shrilmp cook faster.

Drain and rinse under cold water immediately.

TO CLEAN COOKED SHRIMP

Slit the shrimp down the back with a sharp knife, and peel off the shell.

Carefully pick out the black vein of the back with the tip of your knife.

Shrimp is ready to prepare for your recipe.

NOTE
Certain dishes (such as Butterfly Shrimp, Shrimp Quiche, etc.) require that the shrimp be shelled and deveined before cooking.

Common sense is your rule with each recipe, since an unattractive black vein or surplus shell will detract from both the taste and appearance of the dish you're serving.

EXTRA LARGE BROILED GULF PRAWNS
with Lemon Beurre Blanc Sauce

Ingredients

lemon *beurre blanc* sauce
20 extra large Gulf
  prawns
1/2 cup oil

SERVES 4

NOTE
To prepare lemon *beurre blanc* sauce (see p. 7) add to the ingredients, one whole lemon. Cut lemon in quarters and cook with sauce, leaving peel on.

TO CLEAN PRAWNS
Remove heads. With sharp kitchen scissors, cut off legs. Leave shell on. Holding prawn with its back side down in the palm of your hand, insert scissors through belly part, splitting through tail. Do not remove tail. Make sure not to cut back part.

TO COOK
Preheat broiler. On greased rack, place prawns belly side up, tail sticking up, making sure they will stay that way while cooking them. Brush with oil. Place under broiler.

Cook for 3 or 4 minutes, making sure not to overcook or char their tails.

Serve with a rice pilaf, arranging pilaf in center and placing prawns around it. Gently spoon some sauce over prawns.

Serve at once.

SCAMPI WITH FRESH LINGUINI, Olive Oil, and Herbs

SERVES 6-8

Cook linguini in boiling salted water. Be careful not to overcook; they should be firm (*al dente*).

Drain and toss with a bit of olive oil to prevent sticking and dryness. Set aside.

In large skillet, using the remaining oil, sauté the garlic and shrimp. Add basil, oregano, parsley, and cook 2 to 3 minutes, until the shrimp begin to curl.

Add the linguini and mix with a fork or tongs. Add the grated pecorino Romano (optional).

Serve the linguini on warm plates and place shrimps on top. Garnish with a leaf of basil or sprig of parsley.

Ingredients

1 lb linguini
40 medium shrimp, shelled and deveined
3 garlic cloves, chopped
1/2 cup olive oil
1 oz fresh basil, chopped
1/2 oz fresh oregano, chopped
1/2 oz fresh parsley, chopped
6 oz grated pecorino Romano (optional)

BAKED SHRIMP-STUFFED AVOCADOS

Ingredients

2 large avocados
2 Tbsp fresh lemon juice
1 tsp salt
4 Tbsp (1/2 stick) butter
4 Tbsp flour
sprinkling of ground
    white pepper
1 cup light cream (or half-
    and-half)
1/4 cup celery, thinly
    sliced and cooked
1 small pimiento, minced
1/2 lb shrimp, cooked,
    shelled, deveined, and
    coarsely chopped
1 Tbsp Cheddar cheese,
    grated (optional)

SERVES 4

Preheat oven to 350 F.

Cut avocados in half lengthwise and remove the pits.

Sprinkle halves with lemon juice and 1/2 tsp of the salt.

Melt butter in the top part of a double boiler.

Blend in flour, pepper, the remaining 1/2 tsp salt, and the cream/ half-and-half.

Cook over boiling water until the mixture thickens, stirring constantly.

Thoroughly mix in celery, pimiento, and shrimp.

Fill avocado halves with shrimp mixture.

Sprinkle with Cheddar cheese. Avocados may be sprinkled with bread crumbs instead of cheese.

Place avocados in a shallow baking dish filled with 1/2 inch water and bake for about 15 minutes.

BEER-BATTER FRIED SHRIMP

SERVES 6

Separate eggs and set whites aside for later use.

Whisk egg yolks, beer, oil, sifted flour, and soy sauce in a bowl.

Blend well until smooth.

Beat egg whites until stiff and fold into the batter.

Hold shrimp by their tails and dip into flour and then into the egg batter, coating well.

Heat oil for deep frying to 375 F in a large, heavy kettle or Dutch oven. A piece of bread dropped into the oil will turn golden brown when the temperature of the oil is just right.

Fry shrimp a few at a time until golden brown, about 4 or 5 minutes.

Drain on paper towels.

Serve hot with a favorite sauce such as Tartar or Cocktail (see pp. 39 and 9).

Ingredients

2 eggs, separated
3/4 cup beer
1 Tbsp corn oil
1 cup sifted flour
1 Tbsp soy sauce
2 lb shrimp, shelled, deveined, and with their tails on
3/4–1 cup flour for dipping shrimp
corn oil for deep frying
Tartar or cocktail sauce

BUTTERFLY SHRIMP

Ingredients

2 egg whites, lightly
   beaten
2 Tbsp ice water
1 tsp salt
sprinkling of ground white
   pepper
3 Tbsp rice flour
1 1/2 lb jumbo shrimp,
   shelled, deveined, and
   split with tails on
peanut oil for deep frying
Tartar sauce (see p. 39) or
   cocktail sauce
   (see p. 9)

SERVES 4-6

Separate egg whites and set yolks aside for another use.

Whisk egg whites, water, salt, and pepper in a bowl.

Blend in the flour and mix until smooth.

Flatten each shrimp into a "butterfly" shape.

Dip into the batter.

Meanwhile, heat oil for deep frying to 375 F in a large, heavy kettle or Dutch oven. A piece of bread dropped into the oil will turn golden brown when the temperature of the oil is just right.

Fry shrimp until golden brown. Drain on paper towels.

Serve hot with a favorite sauce such as Tartar or cocktail.

SHRIMP CAKES

SERVES 3-4

Melt butter in a large, heavy saucepan.

Add onion and cook over low heat until soft.

Stir in flour, mustard, cream, salt, and pepper. Continue stirring until mixture is smooth and begins to thicken.

Mix the shrimp in well.

Pour into a bowl, cover tightly, and refrigerate for 1 hour.

When shrimp mixture has chilled, form into medium-size patties.

Dip patties into beaten egg and then into cracker crumbs, coating evenly and well.

Heat oil in a large, heavy skillet until just sizzling.

Fry shrimp until golden brown and crispy on both sides, turning carefully with a spatula.

Remove patties from the skillet and drain on a paper towel. Serve with any favorite mayonnaise or tomato sauce.

Ingredients

2 Tbsp (1/4 stick) sweet butter
1 small onion, minced
3 Tbsp all-purpose flour
1 tsp Dijon mustard
1 cup light cream
Salt to taste
sprinkling of ground white pepper
1 lb shrimp, cooked, shelled, deveined, and coarsely chopped
1 egg, beaten
1 1/2 cups cracker crumbs, finely crumbled
3/4–1 cup peanut oil
mayonnaise (see p. 23) or tomato sauce (see p. 40)

SHRIMP DE JONGHE

Ingredients

8 Tbsp (1 stick) sweet
   butter
1 small onion, minced
1 garlic clove, minced or
   mashed
1 tsp salt
sprinkling of fleshly
   ground white pepper
1/2 cup Sherry
2 Tbsp fresh parsley,
   minced
2 lb shrimp, cooked,
   shelled, and deveined
3/4 cup fine bread
   crumbs

SERVES 4

Preheat oven to 350 F.

Melt butter in a large, heavy skillet or saucepan. Add onion, garlic, salt, and pepper.

Sauté until onion is golden.

Add Sherry.

Mix in shrimp and parsley and stir well. Arrange shrimp in a shallow casserole.

Pour the butter mixture over all.

Sprinkle with bread crumbs and bake for about 15 minutes or until crumbs are golden brown.

SHRIMP IN DILL BUTTER

SERVES 4

Heat butter with salt, pepper, and dill in a large, heavy skillet until hot, but not sizzling.

Add shrimp and sauté for 3 to 5 minutes, or just until they turn pink.

NOTE
Shrimp may be served on thin slices of toasted French bread as an interesting base, or on rice if you prefer.

Ingredients

8 Tbsp (1 stick) sweet butter
1 tsp salt
sprinkling of ground white pepper
2 Tbsp fresh dill, finely chopped (or dillweed may be used instead)
2 lb shrimp, shelled and deveined

FRIED SHRIMP IN BEER BATTER with Coconut Dip

Ingredients

3 eggs, separated
1 cup beer
1 Tbsp oil
1 cup flour
2 lb medium or large
   shrimp, shelled,
   deveined, and with
   their tails on
1 cup flour for dipping
   shrimp
1 cup shredded coconut
vegetable oil for frying
Tartar sauce (see p. 39)

SERVES 4

In a bowl, whisk together egg yolks, beer, oil, and flour.

Blend until they are smooth. Beat egg whites until they are stiff and fold into the batter.

Hold shrimps by their tails and dip them into flour and then into the beer batter, coating well.

At this point, if desired, press shrimps into shredded coconut to cover.

In a large, heavy kettle or Dutch oven, heat oil for deep frying.

Fry shrimp on medium heat, a few at a time, until they are golden brown, about 4 or 5 minutes.

Drain on paper towels.

Serve hot with Tartar sauce.

FUSILLI WITH GRILLED SHRIMP
and Sundried Tomatoes

SERVES 4

Cook fusilli until *al dente* and drain.

In sauté pan place oil, garlic, basil, sundried tomatoes and shrimp.

Cook for 2 minutes and add fusilli.

Cook for an additional 1–2 minutes.

Serve and garnish with fresh basil leaves.

Ingredients

1 lb fusilli
6 oz sundried tomatoes
16 large shrimp, cleaned
1 Tbsp fresh basil,
    chopped
1/2 Tbsp garlic, chopped
2 olive oil
salt and pepper to taste
4 fresh basil leaves

SHRIMP JAMBALAYA

Ingredients

4 slices bacon, finely chopped
1 Tbsp all-purpose flour
1 thick slice ham (about 1 lb, preferably smoked), diced
1 small onion, coarsely chopped
2 garlic cloves, minced or mashed
1 small green pepper, diced
2 lb shrimp, shelled and deveined
4 medium-large tomatoes (about 1 1/2–2 cups), peeled and coarsely chopped
pinch of cayenne
1 bay leaf
1 cup raw rice
1 tsp salt
ground black pepper to taste
1 tsp chili powder
1 cup boiling water

SERVES 8

Sauté bacon in a large, heavy kettle until most of the fat cooks out.

Slowly stir the flour and brown in the bacon fat.

Add ham, onion, garlic, green pepper, and shrimp.

Continue sautéing until onion is golden.

Add tomatoes, cayenne, bay leaf, rice, salt, pepper, and chili powder.

Mix gently but well.

Pour in boiling water, about 1 cup or just enough to moisten the jambalaya.

Cover and simmer over low heat until rice is tender. Fluff once or twice with a fork.

Be sure the jambalaya has enough water so that rice just absorbs the moisture. Add more boiling water if necessary.

The mixture should be on the firm side and not soupy.

SHRIMP L'ORANGE

SERVES 4-6

Mix juices, Sherry, salt, pepper, and Tabasco in a large bowl.

Add shrimp and toss lightly to distribute the flavors.

Cover tightly and refrigerate overnight.

Drain off the marinade and set aside for later use.

Heat butter in a large, heavy skillet until hot but not sizzling.

Add shrimp and sauté for 3 to 5 minutes, or just until they turn pink.

Remove shrimp from skillet with a slotted spoon, set aside, and keep warm.

Stir flour into the butter in the skillet and blend well. Add the marinade slowly, stirring after each addition.

Simmer over low heat, stirring constantly, until the sauce is smooth and beginning to thicken. Pour the sauce over shrimp before serving. Garnish with fresh parsley.

NOTE
Saffron rice is a good accompaniment for this dish.

Ingredients

1 cup fresh orange juice
1 cup fresh grapefruit juice
1 tsp fresh lemon juice
1 Tbsp Sherry
2 tsp salt
sprinkling of ground white pepper
dash of Tabasco sauce
1 1/2–2 lb shrimp, shelled and deveined
6 Tbsp (3/4 stick) butter
3 Tbsp flour
1 Tbsp fresh parsley
saffron rice (optional)

SHRIMP HAWAIIAN

Ingredients

1 cup heavy cream
1 tsp salt
sprinkling of ground black
    pepper.
1 1/2 lb jumbo shrimp,
    shelled and deveined
    (shrimp also may be
    slit as for Butterfly
    Shrimp (see p. 162)
1 cup all-purpose flour
2 eggs, beaten
1 cup flaked coconut,
    finely chopped
corn oil for deep frying
chutney

SERVES 4

Pour cream into a large bowl and season with salt and pepper.

Marinate shrimp in the cream, tightly covered, for 1 hour in the refrigerator.

Pour off cream and set aside for another use. Note that the cream would be excellent for a cream soup or sauce.

Dip shrimp first in flour, then in eggs, and then in coconut, coating well.

Heat oil for deep frying to 375 F in a large, heavy kettle or Dutch oven A piece of bread dropped into the oil will turn golden brown when the temperature of the oil is just right.

Fry shrimp a few at a time until golden brown, about 4 or 5 minutes. Drain on paper towels.

Serve side dishes of chutney or a favorite sauce with the shrimp.

SHRIMP CREOLE

SERVES 6

Sauté onion, pepper, and celery in oil in a large, heavy kettle or Dutch oven for 2 or 3 minutes.

Add garlic. Cook 1 minute.

Add tomatoes, salt, pepper, thyme and Tobasco. Simmer over low heat for about 20 minutes. Cook 5 minutes.

Heat 2 Tbsp of oil until hot. Add shrimp and cook 2 minutes.

Add creole sacue and simmer 2 minutes.

NOTE:
The creole is usually served on rice or toast points.

Ingredients

1 Tbsp garlic, minced
1 medium-large onion, finely chopped
1 medium-large green pepper, diced1 large stalk celery, diced
2 Tbsp +1/4 cup olive oil
4 medium-large tomatoes (1 1/2–2 cups) coarsely chopped
1 Tbsp fresh thyme, chopped
1/2 tsp salt or to taste
sprinkling of ground black pepper
1 cup frozen okra, sliced
pinch of cayenne
10 squirts of Tobasco
2 lb shrimp, shelled and deveined

SHRIMP QUICHE

Ingredients

Pastry for a 1 crust 9-inch pie
1lb small shrimp, shelled and deveined
6 oz Muenster cheese, finely shredded (or another cheese of your choice, such as Swiss, Monterey Jack, etc.)
4 eggs
1 cup light cream
1 cup half-and-half
1 tsp salt
generous sprinkling of ground white pepper
2 large tomatoes, peeled and cut in thick slices

SERVES 4

Preheat oven to 450 F.

Line a 9-inch pie plate with a favorite rich pastry crust.

Bake for 5 minutes.

Remove crust from oven and add shrimp and cheese.

Thoroughly whisk eggs, cream, half-and-half, salt, and pepper together in a large bowl.

Pour over shrimp and cheese and return to the oven. Bake for about 10 or 15 minutes.

Reduce heat to 350 F and bake for about 15 to 20 minutes more, until a knife inserted in the quiche comes out clean.

Cut in wedges and serve with thick slices of tomato on the side.

SHRIMP WIGGLE

SERVES 4

Melt butter in a large, heavy skillet or Dutch oven. Add onion and sauté until golden.

Lightly mix in peas, tomatoes, tomato juice, salt, pepper, rosemary, and cayenne. Heat just to boiling. Reduce heat and simmer for about 5 minutes.

Mix cornstarch with just enough liquid from the skillet to blend.

Stir gently but thoroughly into the sauce.

Add a bit more cornstarch (mixing it first with cooled liquid from the skillet) if you want a thicker sauce. Add shrimp.

Heat for 2 or 3 minutes, just until the shrimp is heated through.

Mix in baking soda and blend well.

Put a handful of oyster crackers in the bottom of each soup bowl and top with the shrimp wiggle.

Sprinkle lightly with paprika to garnish.

Ingredients

- 4 Tbsp (1/2 stick) sweet butter
- 1 medium-large onion, minced
- 1 cup fresh green peas, shelled and cooked
- 2 medium-large tomatoes (about 1–1 1/4 cups), peeled and coarsely chopped
- 1/2 cup tomato juice
- 1 tsp salt
- sprinkling of ground black pepper
- pinch of rosemary
- pinch of cayenne
- 1/2 Tbsp cornstarch
- 1 1/2 lb shrimp, cooked, shelled, deveined, and cut in half (if shrimp are on the small side, you may prefer to leave them whole)
- 1/2 tsp baking soda
- oyster crackers
- paprika

SAUTÉED SHRIMP
with Julienne of Leek in White Wine Cream Sauce with Truffles

Ingredients

2 lb large shrimp, peeled, cleaned, and deveined
4 oz clarified butter
4 oz dry white wine
1 pt heavy cream or half-and-half
3 julienned leeks, white part only
1 black truffle, slivered
salt and pepper to taste

SERVES 4

Sauté shrimp over high heat in clarified butter. Cook only until they begin to curl and turn pink. Do not overcook!

Remove shrimps and set them aside in warm place.

Deglaze saucepan with white wine and add julienne of leeks and heavy cream.

Continue cooking until the mixture has reduced to a sauce of medium thickness.

Add shrimps along with any juices they have released. Mix thoroughly to coat all the shrimps with the sauce.

Serve immediately by dividing shrimps onto serving plates and spooning sauce and leeks over top.

Garnish with slivers of truffle (optional). Salt and pepper to taste.

THE FISH

OF THE GRAND CENTRAL

OYSTER BAR

- VARIETIES

- BUYING AND PREPARING

- PLANKED FISH

- SMOKED FISH

- FISH RECIPES

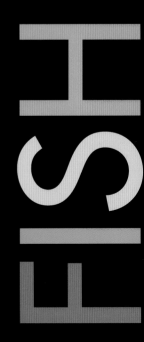
FISH

THE FISH
OF THE GRAND CENTRAL
OYSTER BAR

The Oyster Bar menu changes daily, depending on what fresh fish is available at the market for that day. Goldeye may be flown in from Lake Winnipeg and pompano and red snapper up from Florida, or halibut and cod trucked down from Massachusetts. Our fish purchasing agent has a "hot line" all over the United States that alerts him to what fish and shellfish are being caught, even as you read this book. For instance, a pre-dawn telephone call from Chatham, Massachusetts, on Cape Cod, may report that a 100-plus-pound halibut has just been pulled aboard on one of the small fishing boats. If the fish is accepted (depending on the restaurant's inventory), hours later the gigantic halibut will roll through Grand Central Station en route to The Oyster Bar—attracting curious commuters on their way to work like some aquatic Pied Piper. Just a few more hours and halibut will be on the menu for lunch and dinner.

The most important rule, whether a fish weighs in at 1 pound or 100 pounds, is that it be absolutely fresh. You can acquire expertise with practice, so that you can buy fresh fish as professionals do. You should be able to walk into a market and immediately make your selection regardless of how varied the choice. Fresh fish will have eyes that are bulging, bright, and clear. There should never be the slightest unnatural odor in the gill area; be sure the gills are not brown and that their color is reddish pink. If you hold a small-to-medium-size fresh fish at the tail, its body will stand straight out without flopping over. The flesh will be firm and elastic enough so that it will spring back when you press it. Above all fresh fish will shine, and that shine is what should capture your eye when you're shopping for the catch of the day.

VARIETIES OF FISH

THE OYSTER BAR serves more than 30 varieties of fish cooked to order, with broiling the most popular method by far. This list will help you to select your own catch of the day to prepare at home. With fast refrigerated transportation, many fresh fish are available all year round to most parts of the United States. Although frozen fish is never served at The Oyster Bar, excellent freezing processes make it possible for seafood lovers to enjoy many varieties of fish that would not ordinarily be available in certain areas. FW and SW indicate whether the fish come from fresh or salt water.

BLUEFISH (SW)

The stout-bodied, delicately flavored bluefish is available year round from the warm waters of the Atlantic and the Gulf. "Blues" winter off the Florida coast and move northward past the Carolinas and Long Island up to Massachusetts during the spring and summer months. The whole fish you'll find in the market will probably weigh between 1 and 2 pounds. Fillets from larger fish are also available.

BROOK TROUT (also Speckled, Rainbow, and Mountain) (FW)

Trout has become so popular in recent years that fish farms specializing in the breeding of trout, particularly small rainbow, have been developed in certain areas. Happily this culinary delicacy with its firm, sweet flesh is now available fresh all year. A quantity of superb quality trout comes from Idaho. Trout thrives in fast-moving, cold and clear fresh water. Small trout average 10 to 12 in long, and are graded in the market according to weight: 8, 10-12, and 14 ounces.

CATFISH (FW)

The catfish may never win a beauty contest—as someone once joked, "The catfish is swimming proof that ugly is only skin deep"—but its firm and flaky meat is light and tasty. As well as being available year round, catfish are international travelers that turn up in waters all over the world. The skinned and dressed fish you select at market will be ideal weight at 1/3 pound, but larger fish are available.

FLOUNDER (Blackback) (SW)

The blackback, also called winter flounder, is thick, meaty, and considered the most flavorful of the flounderfamily. This fish is taken from North and mid-Atlantic waters and the Chesapeake Bay, and is available all year. Winter flounder weigh between 1–2 pounds.

FLOUNDER (Summer Flounder, Fluke) (SW)

As its name implies, the summer flounder, also called fluke, is plentiful during the summer months along the mid-Atlantic Coast. The fish is flat and white-meated, and has an excellent flavor. Your purchase will weigh between 1 and 5 pounds.

GOLDEYE (FW)

Of the more than 400,000 pounds of goldeye taken from Canada's Lake Winnipeg and smoked (the hot-smoking process turns the fish a magnificent reddish color) every year, only a small percentage reaches the United States. Goldeye is not available in seafood markets here, and many people who have acquired a taste for the rich, smoky flavor of the fish come to The Oyster Bar just to enjoy this delicacy.

GROUPER (Florida Red) (SW)

The grouper is a member of the delicious sea bass family, and the Florida red is found in the Atlantic waters south of Virginia. Adult fish can weigh as much as 50 pounds or more, but average market weight is between 5-15 pounds. Unless you're feeding 8 or more people, you'll be buying fillets and steaks. The red grouper has always been an underrated fish, even though it compares favorably with red snapper and is less expensive. Available year round.

HADDOCK (SW)

The haddock is a native of North Atlantic waters from Nova Scotia to North Carolina, and is a close but smaller relative of the cod. Average market weight is between 2 1/2 and 3 pounds. The fish is a year round favorite that can be prepared in a variety of ways. When it's smoked the firm, pleasant-tasting white meat of the haddock becomes finnan haddie.

HAKE (SW)

Whole hake is easily identified in the market by its streamlined body, two dorsal fins, large eyes, and a feeler, but it's usually sold in fillet form. The soft, white flesh and delicate flavor of the hake make it an ideal substitute for either haddock or cod, and some people prefer it to both. The fish is available year round from the waters of the North Atlantic.

HALIBUT (Eastern) (SW)

The gigantic halibut weighing 100 pounds (and some tipping the scales up to 250 pounds) is available all year, but the most plentiful catch off the New England coast is taken from March to October. The flaky-textured firm and white delicately flavored meat is ideal for steaks, and you can also buy pieces of halibut that can be used for everything from chowders to bouillabaisse.

LING (Ling Cod) (SW)

Even though ling is also called ling cod, the fish is not related to the cod. It has its own unusual and distinctive flavor. Ling is native to the waters of the North and South Pacific, and can be purchased year round. Average weight of a dressed fish is about 2 pounds, and the larger ling over 4 pounds are sold filleted or prepared as steaks.

MACKEREL (Boston) (SW)

There are more than 20 different varieties of mackerel, and the Boston mackerel served at The Oyster Bar is one of the most popular. The season in the Northeast Atlantic from April to November is eagerly awaited by everyone who appreciates fresh mackerel. Average weight for this firm and rather oily fish that has a rich and distinctive flavor is 1 1/2 to 2 pounds. Mackerel is sold either whole or in fillets.

PERCH (Ocean) (SW)

Rosefish, redfish, and red perch are other names for what you'll be buying in a fish market as ocean perch. This fish is available year round in deep waters from Greenland south to New Jersey. Average weight is 1/2 to 1 pound and the larger fish are filleted. The ocean perch has firm, slightly coarse flesh and a bland flavor that lends itself perfectly to rich sauces.

PERCH (Yellow) (FW)

Yellow perch are plentiful year round in lakes and rivers throughout the northeastern United States from the Great Lakes to the upper Mississippi Valley. Transplanting has extended their waters to the Ohio River and some western states. Blue pike, yellow pike, and sauger belong to the yellow perch family and are not pike relatives as their name implies. Yellow perch weigh less than a pound, rarely more, and the small fish are marketed whole. Their flavor is excellent and the meat is firm and white.

POMPANO (SW)

This choice fish is considered an epicurean delight for its rich white meat and exquisite flavor. Pompano is available year round from the South Atlantic waters off the Florida coast and in the Gulf of Mexico. Average weight is between 1 1/2 and 3 pounds.

PORGY (SW)

Ever since Porgy sang to Bess, this little fish has become a household name. The porgy swims the Atlantic Coast from South Carolina to Maine, and in New England is also known as the scup. Porgies weigh from 3/4 up to 4 pounds, and their meat is flaky, tender, and flavorful. Available all year.

RED SNAPPER (SW)

You can't miss this colorful fish in your seafood market's display and you won't want to—especially if you feel like splurging a bit, since this is not an inexpensive fish. Red snapper is one of the finest delicacies the sea has to offer, and many people consider it the filet mignon of the fish world. The flavor of red snapper's succulent white meat is indescribable. The fish are native to the South Atlantic and Gulf of Mexico waters, and are available year round. The ideal weight for a red snapper is between 8 and 12 pounds, if you want fillets. Otherwise, whole fish between 1 and 3 pounds are available.

SALMON (Chinook) (SW)

The largest and perhaps best known of the 5 North Pacific salmon, Chinook is served at The Oyster Bar. This and other varieties of salmon may be sold in your area's fish markets.

Chinook is Indian for "spring," when the salmon begins its run from the open seas to the fresh water of Oregon's Columbia River, where it's taken. Adult salmon ranges in weight from 6 to 60 pounds, and up. The season is from May to October, although other kinds of salmon are available year round. Most people are familiar with the canned and smoked versions of the fish, but fresh salmon is a special treat with its rich, firm, and reddish meat. Salmon steaks cut 1 1/2 inches thick are the most common way the fish is sold, although some markets offer fillets.

SCROD (Boston) (SW)

Scrod is the baby aristocrat of the cod family, and any cod that weighs 2 1/2 pounds or under qualifies as scrod. These tasty little cod with their firm, flaky white flesh are plentiful year round in New England waters and from the Grand Banks of Newfoundland, Young haddock and pollock of the same size are also called scrod.

SEA BASS (Black) (SW)

The sea bass is a relative of the grouper and jewfish, among other members of a large fish family. They're taken year round from the mid-Atlantic Coast, and market weights range from 1/2 to 5 pounds. Sea bass are sold whole, or cut into steaks and fillets. Their meat is lean, juicy, and delicately flavored. The black sea bass served at The Oyster Bar is native to Atlantic waters, but a similar sea bass is available on the West Coast.

SHAD (SW)

Shad is a seasonal fish available from January to May. During January the fish are plentiful off the Florida coast. The shad runs begin in Georgia in February, and the best shad is taken from South Carolina in April as the fish swim up the coast through the Chesapeake Bay and into New Jersey. Shad is also available on the Pacific Coast. Weight ranges from 1 1/2 to 8 pounds, and since the fish is so bony, fillets are sold in markets instead of the whole or dressed fish. The flesh of the shad is oily and tasty, and shad roe—which may be purchased separately—is considered one of the great gourmet delicacies.

SHARK (Mako) (SW)

Excitement and curiosity about sharks have sometimes obscured the fact that the big fish, especially the mako shark, compares favorably with swordfish in texture and flavor. It's also much less expensive than swordfish. Mako sharks are found in the warm waters of the Atlantic from about mid-June on into September. You don't have to concern yourself with weight (which can range from 60 to over 1200 pounds) when purchasing shark, since your market will have prepared steaks, fillets, and pieces whenever the fish is available. Other species of shark are available on the West Coast year round.

SMELT (FW)

Smelt is an economical dish, with 8 to 12 fish to the pound and very little waste. Most people like smelt broiled or fried crisp, and the meat is rich and has a slightly sweet, delicious flavor. Thousands of these tiny fish are scooped up by the basketful every year during the smelt runs in the Great Lakes tributary streams from Labrador to New York. The smelt season is from September to May.

SOLE (Lemon and Gray) (SW)

Sole is the most popular fish served in the United States today, perhaps because it is so adaptable. From perfectly broiled for a simple meal, to elegantly sauced and garnished for a classic banquet, sole has become a staple of American seafood cuisine. Both lemon and gray sole have lean, white meat and a delicate pleasing flavor that seems to appeal to everyone. Sole is available year round, and is sold whole and in fillets. The average fish weighs about 4 pounds for lemon sole and 2 pounds for gray sole.

SPEARING (SW) (see Whitebait for details)

Spearing are large whitebait—which means they're about 1/2 to 1 inch longer than their little relatives.

SPOT (SW)

This delicately flavored little fish, weighing an average of 1/2 to 1 pound, is taken from the mid- and South-Atlantic and the Chesapeake Bay all year. Unfortunately, spot has been overlooked in favor of some of the other smaller fish, and may have to be ordered specially from your market. Spots are usually sold whole, and they're worth getting to know if you've never tried them.

SQUID (SW)

This distant relative to the octopus is more popular abroad than in the United States. The squid's average weight is from 6 ounces to a pound, and length is about 5 to 10 inches. Your fish market will sell them fully dressed and ready to fry or sauté. Squid is plentiful year round in the Atlantic from Cape May to Labrador, and most squid fanciers agree that the sweet taste has to be acquired.

STRIPED BASS (SW)

This big daddy of the bass family, sometimes called black rockfish, is taken off the Atlantic Coast all year and in the Chesapeake Bay from mid-summer into the winter months. Weight ranges from about 2 pounds up to a 50-pounder (that might be fun to catch but won't be worth eating). Striped bass is sold whole or in fillets. The meat is lean, juicy, and, as with all bass, of excellent flavor.

STURGEON (SW)

The Atlantic Ocean sturgeon, which is available on and off year round from North Carolina up to the New England coast, can run up to 600 pounds and more. The fish is sold in fillets, steaks, and by the piece. It's excellent for stews and chowders, and when broiled its firm white meat is a bit similar to halibut in texture but does have its own unique flavor.

SWORDFISH (SW)

Swordfish range in weight from 50 to 600 pounds, and are taken in the Atlantic from Key West to Nova Scotia. The peak season is from July to September, when the water temperature is ideal and the big fish cruise up the coast from Montauk Point in Long Island to Hyannis, Massachusetts. The Oyster Bar buys only swordfish that have been harpooned, since the fish are taken fresh from the water immediately. The long-lining method of catching swordfish with baited hooks means that the fish may be in the water for a day or two before it's pulled in. Steaks are the form in which you'll purchase swordfish at market, and you can usually have them cut in any desired thickness. The meat is firm, slightly oily, and richer in flavor than halibut.

TUNA (SW)

Canned tuna is a household staple, but an interesting treat is fresh tuna steak when it's available from July to October on the East Coast, and from May to December on the West Coast. Tuna can weigh 1500 pounds or more, although the smaller West Coast albacore—the only true white meat tuna—averages 8 pounds and up. The light meat tuna has an oily texture and a robust flavor; the albacore is more delicate. Tuna steaks may have to be ordered, since they're not generally available in most fish markets.

WEAKFISH (Gray Sea Trout) (SW)

The weakfish or gray sea trout bears no similarity to its freshwater relative in either taste or appearance. Weakfish are taken from mid-Atlantic waters all year, and in abundance from North Carolina fisheries. Average weight is from 1 to 6 pounds, and the fish are sold whole, dressed, or in fillets. The meat is tender and has a good flavor and soft texture.

WHITEBAIT (SW)

Gourmets temporarily turned ichthyologists have variously credited the minnow-like whitebait with being a member of the herring family, an exotic species, the undeveloped offspring of disparate parents. Whatever the answer, these translucent greenish little fish, measuring 1 to 1 1/4 inches, are fine eating. Whitebait season is from September to April on the East Coast, and a quantity of the fish are taken off Point Judith in Rhode Island. Whitebait are best fried and served crisp.

WHITEFISH (FW)

The versatile whitefish comes to The Oyster Bar from the Great Lakes, and is also taken from small lakes in many parts of the United States and Canada, especially Manitoba and Alberta. The whitefish does double duty both as an excellent smoked fish widely available in the East and Midwest, and as a fine fish for sautéeing. Whitefish roe makes a kind of caviar when lightly salted, and it's frequently available in fish markets. Market weight for whitefish is from 2 to 6 pounds, and they're sold whole or in fillets.

WHITING (Silver Hake) (SW)

Whiting or silver hake is available year round, but the fish is most plentiful in the spring and fall off the coast from Virginia to New England. Whiting is very popular for its soft, white, and delicately flavored meat, and frozen fillets are shipped all over the United States. Most of us have eaten whiting as the "fish" part of the classic "fish and chips" dish. Average weight is between 1/2 and 3 pounds. Smaller whiting are sold whole, but the larger fish are cut into fillets.

WOLFFISH (LOUP DE MER) (SW)

The Oyster Bar was the first seafood house in New York to introduce wolffish, or Loup de Mer, so don't be surprised if you have trouble finding it in your fish market. Loup is also a great delicacy in Europe, and at times it's more expensive there than lobster. The wolffish is fierce in appearance, but otherwise it's a gourmet delight. Wolffish feeds primarily on lobster, crab, and other crustaceans, which accounts for its superb flavor. Its white meat is firm, sweet, and similar to haddock in both texture and flavor. Wolffish season is from October to May in the North Atlantic from North Carolina to Cape Cod, with the catch most abundant in the spring. Average weight is about 8 pounds, and (if you can find it) the fish is sold dressed, in fillets, and in steaks.

BUYING AND PREPARING FISH

If you're a wise shopper you'll get to know the owner of your fish market; don't be afraid to browse and ask him questions. Establish your own "hot line" with the man who runs a good seafood market, and who will be glad to advise you about quality and what fish are the best buys in season for your area. He can help you select the right fish to buy and tell you how much you'll need for a particular recipe, and of course he'll prepare your selection to order for you. (We refer all do-it-yourselfers to any other seafood cookbook that goes into detail about the cleaning and dressing of fish, since here we'll leave the job to the professionals). Many people don't realize that if you're anywhere near the ocean, a bay, lake, river, etc., the freshest of fish can often be bought right on the docks or from the boats as the fishermen bring in their catch. This is the ideal way to have first pick of the catch of the day! Fish are prepared and sold at market in a number of ways, generally depending on the size of the fish.

Whole (or round) are usually small fish that are sold whole as they come from the water.

Drawn fish have only the entrails removed.

Dressed fish have entrails, head, tail, and fins removed. The larger dressed fish such as swordfish, halibut, salmon, etc. are sold in cross-sections, or steaks, cut 1 inch or more thick. Sometimes they're also sold in large pieces. The smaller dressed fish are split along the back or the belly and may have the backbone removed.

Fillets are the meaty boneless sides of the fish that have been cut lengthwise from the backbone and skinned. When the two sides are left joined by the skin they're called "butterfly" or double fillets.

Sticks are skinless 1–1 1/2-inch slices of fish that have been cut crosswise or lengthwise from fillets and steaks.

When buying fish you have to consider the variety and price range available; the varying amount of waste involved, depending on how you purchase the fish; whether the fish is lean (such as halibut) or fat (such as pompano), since a fat fish will generally stretch further than a lean one. And finally, your recipe. Obviously a fish that has been breaded, stuffed, or richly sauced will not have to be as large to serve 4 or 6 persons as one that is simply broiled. When it comes to quantity, fish is a bit trickier to buy than meat. Here your fish market will be helpful in suggesting the amount to buy for the number of persons to be served. There's a general rule for purchasing fish that you can use and adapt for yourself, depending on the appetites of family and guests. If you're buying fish:

Whole (or Round): allow 1 pound per person
Drawn: allow 3/4 to 1 pound per person
Dressed: allow 1/2 pound per person
Fillets and Sticks: allow 1/3 to 1/2 pound per person

One of the great joys of eating seafood is a sizzling, perfectly broiled fish. Nothing dulls the appetite faster than a limp and lukewarm fish brought to the table—regardless of how beautifully it may be garnished and served. You have to work quickly when broiling fish, using a sixth sense of timing that will let you know the exact moment your fish is cooked to perfection. A properly broiled fish should be juicy, never overcooked or underdone, and an appetizing golden brown when served. Your sixth sense of timing will get foolproof with practice, and the rest is up to a good hot broiler with an even temperature and, of course, your fish.

The Oyster Bar has the advantage of professional broilers and other equipment, as most seafood restaurants do, but you can satisfactorily duplicate these conditions at home. Your broiler should always be preheated at 550 F or "broil" (follow any special broiling instructions for your stove) for at least 10 minutes, and preferably for 20 minutes. When a broiler rack is hot, brush it with canola oil. Sprinkle the rack with fine cracker crumbs to keep the fish from sticking. Place the fish on the rack (the skin side is always placed down) and brush the top with canola oil. Slide the broiler rack under the flame so that the fish is about 3 inches below the heat. It's not necessary to turn the fish, since the preheated broiler rack should sufficiently brown the underside. Lean fish is usually basted once during broiling, but this is optional. Lean fish include cod, flounder, haddock, swordfish, and perch. It's not necessary to baste fat fish, such as mackerel, pompano, salmon, tuna, etc., since they have a sufficient amount of fat for broiling. It's better to have a fish slightly undercooked than to overcook it. Since fish require intense heat and such a short time to broil, you'll find that they'll continue to cook a bit even after you've removed them from the broiler to a preheated serving dish. You can serve split fish, fillets, and sticks after 6 to 8 minutes of broiling, and fish steaks and whole fish after 8 to 10 minutes. Use a spatula or tongs to lift fish carefully from the broiler.

Handle fish very gently, since bruised or punctured flesh and skin will deteriorate rapidly.

When cooking a whole fish, leave the head on if possible. It can always be removed later, if you prefer, before the fish is served. Leaving the head on seals in juices and keeps the fish moist. Never rinse fish under running water. Dip the fish in icy, salted water instead, and pat dry. Always substitute a fat fish for another fat fish, and a lean fish for another lean one in any recipe. Slightly moistened salt applied to the hands and rinsed off with warm water will remove any fish odor from your skin, and rubbed on pots, knives, and other kitchen utensils— followed by a thorough rinsing with hot water—it will remove any fish smell that remains. Oven pans, dishes, skillets, trays, etc. should be soaked in hot, salted water as soon as they cool.

If you're a fisherman/woman yourself, chances are you know how to clean your catch. At the risk of bringing on a basketful of complaints from fish markets all over the United States: If someone gives you a freshly caught fish or you've purchased one, and you don't want to or don't know how to clean it yourself, you don't have to hesitate about asking your fish market to do the job for you. Leave the fish and pick it up later if they're busy at the market. The cost of cleaning and dressing will be nominal, and perhaps nothing if you're a regular customer. If you expect to have freshly caught fish often, you should be able to make some special arrangement with your fish market.

Use only the finest quality oil, wine, butter, herbs, etc. in cooking fish. Inferior quality products will let you know immediately that you're doing something wrong. A fine fish deserves fine ingredients in any recipe.

A small, whisk-type brush is ideal for distributing oil or butter evenly over fish. A long, two-tined fork will work as your "magic wand" when you're checking to see if fish flakes easily. It will cause less breakage in the fish, too. Create your own eye-catching garnishes that are so important to the attractive serving of fish dishes, and don't be afraid to experiment with something different.

Here are just a few ideas to get you started:

Dip cherry tomatoes in seasoned salt. Fill large raw mushroom caps with Tartar Sauce. Fill lettuce cups with cocktail Sauce. Use (warmed when the sauce is hot) scooped-out tomatoes, cucumbers, squash, zucchini, green peppers, etc. as "serving dishes" for your seafood sauces.

PLANKED FISH

Planked fish are impressive, and always elegant for special occasions. In fact they're so easy to do, you don't even need a special occasion! A whole fish is best for planking, but there's no reason you can't use split fish, steaks, fillets, and even sticks. First you'll need a good hardwood plank made from well-seasoned oak, hickory, or ash. It will be 1 to 1 1/2 inches thick, and do buy the best one you can find because you'll have it forever. It will be oval and have a pine tree design carved down its length and a shallow groove around its edge to hold juices. Some planks have a shallow depression at one end instead of the outer groove. Before you use your new plank, you'll want to season it further by brushing it with corn oil and putting it in the oven (preheated to 225 F) for 1 hour. Whenever you cook on it, always be sure that any exposed part of the plank is well oiled. It should never be used to cook anything except fish.

To cook on the plank: put the cold plank in the oven and heat it for 10 minutes at 350 F. Remove the plank from the oven and coat it.

Fish will bake in about 50 minutes or 1 hour in the 350 F oven; split fish, steaks, fillets, and sticks will take less time. As with broiling, when the fish flakes easily with a fork and is nicely browned, it's ready to serve.

SMOKED FISH

With the increasing popularity of smoked fish in the United States, The Oyster Bar has installed its own wood-smoking ovens. The ovens are completely smoke-controlled so that there are no environmental protection problems. Smoked salmon is by far the most popular, but other varieties of smoked fish can be had at The Oyster Bar, and adventurous diners are experimenting with and apparently enjoying them. Smoked fish can also be ordered in advance from the restaurant to take home. The fish is placed in a special marinade for 6 to 8 hours before smoking, and both the marinade and the smoking time depend on the fish selected. The smoking process (again, depending on the choice of fish) is anywhere from 16 to 40 hours.

PANFRIED ARCTIC CHAR
with Red and Black Caviar

Ingredients

4 fillets of Arctic char
(boneless, about 8 oz
each
beurre blanc (see p. 7)
4 oz clarified butter for
sautéing
salt and pepper to taste
2 oz black caviar
2 oz red caviar
flour for dredging

SERVES 4

Proceed to make caviar *beurre blanc* , adding 1 oz of each caviar. Set aside in a warm place for future use.

Preheat the sauté pan. Add clarified butter.

Dredge fillets in flour, shaking off excess. Salt and pepper to taste.

Sauté fillets, SKIN SIDE UP (very important, otherwise fish will curl), for about 3 minutes.Flip fillets over. Reduce heat and continue to cook for another 2 minutes.

Remove fish from skillet, place onto warm serving plate and spoon some of the *beurre blanc* sauce on top and add some of the 2 caviars for decoration. Serve very hot with a boiled potato or rice pilaf and steamed *haricots verts*.

POMPEDOUR OF BLACK SEA BASS

SERVES 4

Slice potatoes 1/8 inch thick. Mix canola oil with clarified butter to prevent potatoes from browning.

Lay out potato slices flat, overlapping one another so that the layer of

potato slices is 4 times the size of each fillet.

Place a fillet in the center of the sliced potatoes and wrap potatoes slices ove, shingling and sealing fillets.

Sauté fillets in oil and clarified butterSKIN SIDE UP over medium heat for about 4 1/2 minutes.

Seal each serving with a brushing of melted butter.

MAKE RED WINE SAUCE
Substitute a Cabernet or Barolo for white wine in the *beurre blanc* recipe.

Panfry each fillet in oil until potatoes are golden brown on both sides. Sauté leeks in 2 oz butter and season with salt and pepper.

Spread 2 oz of red wine sauce on plate and spread out evenly. Add 1/4 cup cooked leeks and place fillet on top of leeks.

Ingredients

4 1 /2 lb black sea bass, cleaned and filleted
4 extra large Idaho potatoes, peeled
1/2 lb (2 sticks) clarified sweet butter
8 oz canola oil
2 oz butter
salt and pepper to taste
4 leeks, white part only
1 oz fresh chives
8 oz red wine sauce (see *beurre blanc* (see p. 7)
salt and pepper

SEA BASS
with Fresh Ginger
and Scallions

Ingredients

4 fillets of sea bass,
approximately 8 to 10
oz each or 8 approxi-
mately 4 oz each
(serving two per
portion)
1 qt of light or heavy
cream
1 bunch of sliced scallions
1 large handful of fresh
grated ginger
1/2 cup of bread crumbs
salt and pepper
to taste
beurre blanc (see p. 7)

SERVES 4

Mix cream, sliced scallions, two-thirds of the grated ginger, salt, and pepper in a shallow dish.

Marinate the fish in the mixture for at least two hours.

Proceed to make the *beurre blanc*, using the remaining fresh ginger in the reduction.

Pre-heat broiler.

Place fish on the broiling rack.

Sprinkle some bread crumbs over each fillet and scoop some ginger and scallions from the marinade and top the dish.

Broil the fish for about 2 to 3 minutes. Finish it in the oven for 3 minutes at 450 F.

When the fish is cooked, handle it very carefully. It will be very delicate. Use a spatula to place it on a plate and arrange the sea bass with a scoop of rice pilaf.

Spoon the ginger *beurre blanc* over the fillets.

Serve at once.

PAN-FRIED FILLET OF SEA BASS
with Peaches, Grapes and Riesling

SERVES 4

Lightly flour sea bass fillet and pan fry in 3 oz oil for 4–5 minutes. Set aside.

In 1 oz canola oil, sauté peaches and grapes for 1 minute.

Add Riesling and reduce for 2 minutes over low heat.

Add butter, stir in well, and serve over fillets.

Salt and pepper to taste.

Ingredients

4 1 1/2 lb black sea bass, filleted and skinned
4 oz flour
4 oz canola oil
2 peaches, peeled and sliced
1 lb white seedless grapes
1 1/2 cups late harvest Riesling
2 Tbsp sweet butter
salt and pepper to taste

BROILED STRIPED BASS
with Montpellier Butter

Ingredients

4 10 oz striped bass fillets
4 oz bread crumbs
2 oz canola oil
Montpellier butter
    (see p. 26)

SERVES 4

Make Montpellier Butter (p. 26).

Season fillets with canola oil and bread crumbs and broil for 6–7 minutes.

Place 2 oz Montpellier butter on top of fish and serve immediately.

BROILED STRIPED BASS
with Sautéed Shiitake Mushrooms

SERVES 4

Preheat broiler and have racks at the ready.

Pat dry fillets, salt and pepper to taste.

Dust with bread crumbs and shake off excess.

Moisten fillets with canola oil

Place fillets on rack (skin side down) and put under broiler (approximately 8 to 10 inches from flame).

Cook fish for 4 minutes, turning once. Continue to cook for another 2 minutes in order to crisp skin.

When fillets are ready, keep in warm place.

Sauté Shiitake in clarified butter, add salt and pepper, minced garlic, and shallots. Cook until mushrooms are tender.

Place fish on serving plates and spoon cooked mushrooms over fillets.

Serve at once.

Ingredients

8 small fillets (2 per person) with the skin on
salt and pepper
bread crumbs, finely crumbled
8 oz fresh Shiitake mushrooms
2 Tbsp clarified butter
2 medium garlic cloves, peeled and minced
2 large shallots, peeled and minced

BROILED FILLET OF BLACK SEA BASS
with Fresh Basil and Roasted Pignoli Nuts

Ingredients

4 fillets of black sea bass
4 oz clarified butter
4 oz pignoli nuts
3 oz fresh basil
unflavored bread crumbs sfor
cooking
salt and pepper to taste

SERVES 4

Preheat broiler and broiling rack.

In a small pan over medium heat, melt butter until it is almost brown

While butter is still sizzling add pignoli nuts. Move pan in a circular motion to avoid burning pignoli nuts. You want them to get golden brown, but be careful, because they burn very easily.

Once the nuts are golden brown, drain them and keep in a warm place. Reserve brown butter.

Separate fresh basil leaves from stalks, discard stalks.

Keep flower bouquets from top of plant for garnishing.

Roll leaves into the shape of a cigar, layering larger leaves on the outside.

With a sharp knife (to avoid bruising), cut into thin strips (chiffonade). Separate thin strips from each other, set aside for garnish.

Pat dry black sea bass fillets and dip into bread crumbs for a light coating and shake off excess.

Place on broiling rack, skin side up.

Broil at a distance of about 4 to 6 in from the heat for
4 minutes.

Turn fish once and continue to broil for another 4
minutes.

When fish is ready, transfer to a warm serving plate,
skin side down.

Arrange fish and place basil bouquet at the top end.

Spoon some pignoli nuts onto the top (it should look
like a small nest).

Spread remaining pignoli nuts over fish, and also
spread basil chiffonade.

Spoon some of the brown butter that you reserved on
top of each fish.

Serve at once.

SAUTÉED COD TONGUES AND CHEEKS
with Fiddlehead Ferns

Ingredients

2 lb mixed cod tongues
     and cheeks, cleaned
     and skinned
flour for dredging
salt and pepper to taste
4 oz clarified butter or
     canola oil for sautéing
1 tsp garlic, minced
1 tsp shallot, minced
1 lb fiddlehead ferns,
     cleaned and trimmed

SERVES 4

Preheat large skillet.

Dredge fish in flour, shake off excess. Season with salt and pepper to taste.

Clear off dirty stem ends first, then steam fiddlehead ferns. Be sure to keep them firm. Set aside.

Add 3 oz butter or oil to skillet. Keep flame high! Add fish to skillet (be careful that it doesn't splatter you).

Cook on one side until golden, approximately 2 minutes. Turn and cook for another 2 to 3 minutes.

Set aside on warm plate.

Wipe skillet clean and use again for sautéing fiddlehead ferns in the remaining butter for 2 minutes, until the ferns are hot.

Add garlic and shallots and cook 1 more minute.

Arrange cheeks and tongues. Serve fiddleheads and fish with white and red bliss potatoes or rice.

COD PORTUGUESE

SERVES 4

Heat oil in a large, heavy skillet.

Add onion, celery, green pepper, and garlic, and sauté for about 3 minutes until onions are tender.

Stir in tomatoes and all seasonings and bring just to a boil.

Reduce heat, cover skillet, and simmer for about 30 minutes.

Stir well, add cod, and cover the fillets with the tomato sauce.

Simmer for about 10 minutes or until fish flakes easily with a fork.

Cut into 4 portions.

Serve immediatley.

Ingredients

1 1/2—2 lb cod fillets
1/4 cup olive oil
1 large onion, finely
    choped
1/2 stalk celery, finely
    chopped
1 large green pepper
    (about 1/2 cup), finely
    chopped
1 large garlic clove, finely
    chopped
5 large tomatoes (2 1/2
    cups), peeled and
    coarsely chopped
1 Tbsp fresh parsley,
    minced
1/2 tsp dried basil
1 bay leaf
1/2 tsp cayenne
pinch of sugar
1 tsp salt
dash of finely ground fresh
    black pepper

CREAMED
FINNAN HADDIE

Ingredients

4 1/2 lb boneless finnan
   haddie (haddock)
1 cup milk
1 bay leaf
pinch of thyme
12 whole black
   peppercorns
1 small onion, finely
   chopped
4 Tbsp (1/2 stick) sweet
   butter
1/2 cup flour
1 cup half-and-half
1/4 cup light cream
pinch of cayenne
2 hard-cooked eggs,
   coarsely chopped
1 large pimiento, finely
   chopped
4 slices white bread,
   toasted

SERVES 4

In a large heavy skillet or saucepan soak finnan haddie in milk with bay leaf, thyme, peppercorns, and onion, for about 1 hour.

Then place over very low heat and simmer for about 10 minutes.

Remove the fish from milk with a slotted spoon.

Strain the milk (discard the seasonings and onion) and set aside.

Flake the finnan haddie. Melt butter in the same heavy skillet or saucepan.

Slowly blend in the flour and gradually add half-and-half and cream, stirring constantly.

Cook over low heat until the sauce begins to thicken. If sauce becomes too thick, add a little of the milk in which the finnan haddie soaked.

Add the flaked fish, cayenne, eggs, and pimiento. Stir until heated through.

Serve over white toast.

STEAMED
FINNAN HADDIE
with Egg Sauce

SERVES 4

Make white wine cream sauce.

Poach finnan haddie in milk for 10 minutes on low heat.

Dry the fillets, place one chopped egg on top of each fillet, and pour 2 oz of sauce over each egg.

Ingredients

4 10 oz smoke (finnan haddie (haddock)
2 cups milk
4 hard-cooked eggs, chopped
8 oz white wine cream sauce (see p. 32)

FISH-AND-CHIPS

Ingredients

4 medium-large potatoes,
  peeled and cut in
  1/2–3/4 in strips
1 qt ice water
corn oil for deep frying
salt and pepper to taste
1 1/2 cups prepared
  pancake mix
1 egg beaten
1 cup milk
2 lb haddock fillets, cut in
  serving pieces
malt vinegar (optional)

SERVES 4

Preheat oven to 200 F.

Soak potato strips in a bowl of ice water for about 15
minutes. Meanwhile in a large, heavy kettle or skillet,
heat oil for deep frying to 375 F .

Pour off ice water from potato strips and drain and pat
dry on paper towels.

Fry potatoes in oi at 275 degreesl for 2-3 minutes, until
they wilt slightly. Be careful not to put so many potatoes
in the oil that the container overflows when the potatoes
give up their water during frying.

Drain on paper towels.

Raise temperature of oil to 375 degrees.

Thoroughly blend pancake mix, egg, and milk into a
smooth batter. Dip fillets into the batter, coating
completely, and drop into the hot oil in which the
potatoes have been fried.

Refry potatoes till golden brown, 4-5 minutes.

Drain on paper towels and serve wilth vilnegar on side.

BROILED WHOLE FLOUNDER with String Beans Paysanne

SERVES 4

Preheat broiler.

Brush fish with clarified butter on both sides. Sprinkle with bread crumbs.

Place fish on broiling rack and broil under high flame for about 4 minutes. Turning once, continue to broil for another 3 or 4 minutes.

Turn off broiler and put rack with fish into the oven at 350 F to continue cooking.

Make string beans *paysanne.*

Boil string beans until tender but not mushy (about 5 minutes). In a sauté pan, reduce heavy cream by one third.

Sauté shallots in another pan in the clarified butter until shallots are soft.

Drain string beans. Add reduced heavy cream.

Add salt and pepper.

Bake fish for approximately 10 minutes longer for a total of about 18 minutes. Check fish for doneness. Serve immediately on warm serving platters with boiled potatoes and string beans *paysanne.*

Ingredients

4 whole flounder, gutted
    and cleaned
2 oz clarified butter
bread crumbs
1/2 lb string beans
1 shallot, chopped fine
4 oz heavy cream
salt and pepper to taste

BROILED FILLET OF RED GROUPER
with Sautéed Snowpeas and Hollandaise Sauce

Ingredients

4 fillets red grouper
bread crumbs

2 ozclarified butter or vegetable oil
48 (12 perserving) snow peas
basic Hollandaise sauce (see p. 20)
salt and pepper to taste

SERVES 4

Preheat broiler.

Steam snowpeas until just soft. Do not overcook them. Rinse in ice cold water to retard discoloring. Drain and set aside at room temperature.

Make Basic Hollandaise sauce (see p. 20).

Set sauce aside at room temperature.

Sprinkle bread crumbs over fish.

Brush fish with butter or oil and place fish on broiler rack.

Broil for about 5 minutes on each side or until done.

Sauté snow peas in remaining butter or oil.

Arrange 12 per serving as a semi-circular fan on the top and bottom of plate (six at the top and six at the bottom).

Place hot fish in between.

Serve at once with Hollandaise sauce on the side.

BROILED STRIPED BASS
with Chanterelles

SERVES 4

Preheat broiler.

Season fillets with bread crumbs and broil for 6-7 minutes.

While the fillets are broiling, sauté in butter and canola oil the shallots, garlic, salt and pepper for 2 minutes and add chanterelles.

Sauté for an additional 3-5 minutes over high heat. Stir constantly.

With a slotted spoon, place the mushrooms and the sauté mixture on top of the fillets and serve.

Salt and pepper to taste.

Ingredients

4 10 oz striped bass fillets
4 oz fine bread crumbs
2 oz canola oil
2 oz clarified butter
  chanterelles
2 shallots, chopped
3 garlic cloves, minced
8 oz fresh, small, cleaned
salt and pepper

HADDOCK SOUFFLÉ

Ingredients

1 pound haddock fillets,
   cooked and flaked
8 oz fresh, small, cleaned
3 Tbsp sweet butter
3 Tbsp flour
1/2 tsp salt
dash of ground white
   pepper
pinch of cayenne
1 cup half-and-half
3 eggs, separated

SERVES 4

Preheat oven to 350 F.

Melt butter in a large heavy saucepan. Slowly blend in flour, salt, pepper, and cayenne over low heat.

Add half-and-half and continue stirring constantly over low heat until mixture is smooth and begins to thicken.

Separate eggs and set whites aside.

Add egg yolks to cream mixture, one at a time, mixing thoroughly after each yolk is added.

Bring mixture just to boiling. Remove from heat and add the cooked and flaked fish.

Set fish mixture aside and let cool. Meanwhile, beat egg whites until they are stiff.

Fold whites into the fish mixture and mix well.
Pour into a lightly buttered casserole (1-1 1/2-qt) and bake for about 40 or 45 minutes until the soufflé is firm and puffy.

NOTE
Cod, flounder, or other white fish fillets may be substituted for the haddock.

BROILED HALIBUT FILLET
with Citrus Beurre Blanc

SERVES 4

Season halibut with bread crumbs and gril in oil for 5–7 minutes or until done.

Make *beurre blanc*.

Make a 1/3 reduction of the *beurre blanc* with sectioned fruit.

Serve with 2 oz of citrus *beurre blanc* and garnish with zest of julienned and blanched fruits.

Ingredients

4 10 oz halibut fillets
4 oz bread crumbs
2 oz olive oil
8 oz citrus *beurre blanc* (see p. 7)
2 oranges, zest and sectioned fruit
2 lemons, zest and sectioned fruit
2 limes, zest and sectioned fruit
1 grapefruit, zest and sectioned fruit

HALIBUT STEAKS DIABLE

Ingredients

2 Tbsp Dijon mustard
1 Tbsp peanut oil
2 Tbsp chili sauce
2 Tbsp horseradish
1 tsp salt
2 garlic cloves, minced
4 halibut steaks (about 2
   lb total)
4 sprigs of parsley
2 lemons, cut in wedges

SERVES 4

Preheat lightly buttered broiler pan for about 10 minutes.

Thoroughly blend all ingredients except halibut steaks, parsley, and lemon.

Spread half the mixture over the 4 steaks and broil for about 4—5 minutes until nicely browned.

Turn fish and spread with the remaining sauce.

Put under the broiler for another 5—6 minutes.

Garnish with sprigs of parsley and lemon wedges before serving.

SESAME CRUSTED HALIBUT MEDALLIONS
with Cilantro Sauce

SERVES 4

beurre blanc and set aside. Keep warm.

Mix Japanese bread crumbs, Old Bay seasoning, and sesame seeds.

Lightly pound halibut medallions.

Flour halibut medallions and dip into beaten eggs then cover with crumb mix.

Pan-fry for 2 minutes or until golden brown.

Serve 2 fillets per portion.

Mix cilantro into *beurre blanc* and serve on top of halibut.

Ingredients
8 3–4 oz halibut
  medallions
2 lb Japanese bread
  crumbs
2 Tbsp Old Bay seasoning
1/4 lb sesame seeds
8 oz flour
2 eggs
8 oz *beurre blanc*
  (see p. 7)
2 oz cilantro

POACHED HALIBUT
with Coriander and Jalepeño Cream Sauce

Ingredients

4 10 oz halibut fillets
6 oz *court bouillon*
     (see p. 11)
jalepeño cream sauce
     (see p. 18)

SERVES 4

Make jalepeño cream sauce (see p. 18).

Poach halibut for 8—10 minutes in the *court bouillon.*

Plate and pour 2 oz of sauce on top of each fillet.

STEAMED HALIBUT FILLETS
on Fresh Spinach with Mousseline Sauce

SERVES 4

Poach halibut fillets in fish stock for 8—10 minutes, remove and pat dry, and top each serving with 2 oz white wine sauce .

Top with 1/4 cup mousseline sauce and glacé under broiler until golden brown.

Serve with spinach that has been sautéed with olive oil, shallots, and salt and pepper to taste.

Ingredients

4 10–oz halibut filets
6 oz fish stock
   (see p. 48)
1/2 cup white wine cream
   sauce (see p. 33)
1/4 cup mousseline sauce
   (see p. 27)
1 lb fresh spinach, cleaned
   well
3 Tbsp olive oil
4 tsp shallots
salt and pepper to taste

PAN-FRIED FILLET OF IMPORTED LAVARET
with Lemon and Capers

Ingredients

4 fillets of lavaret, skinless
    and boneles)
flour for dredging
salt and pepper to taste
2 lemons
2 oz clarified butter or oil
2 Tbsp salted butter
1 oz non-pareil capers

SERVES 4

Prepare lemons by peeling all rind and cutting the section from each lemon. Remove seeds. Keep on the side for future use.

Dredge fish fillets in flour, shake off excess. Add salt and pepper.

In a preheated sauté pan or skillet, add clarified butter and, over high heat, sauté fillets for about 3 minutes.

Turn fish once and continue to sauté for another 3 minutes, until fish is golden brown.

Remove fish from skillet and place on warm serving plates.

Drain used clarified butter and in the same HOT skillet add salted butter.

When butter is brown, remove from heat, add capers, and lemon segments. and generously spoon over fish.

Serve very hot.

MEDALLIONS OF LOTTE (Monkfish) with Egg Noodles and Saffron Sauce

SERVES 4

Preheat broiler.

Season lotte with bread crumbs and oil.

Broil fish for 12 minutes or until done.

Remove to cutting board and slice into medallions. Keep warm.

Make saffron sauce (see p. 33).

Cook noodles to desired doneness and mix with melted butter.

Place a small amount of egg noodles in center of each plate and 4 lotte medallions around the outside of the noodles.

Top with saffron sauce and garnish with chopped parsley or chives.

NOTE
A variation on this recipe is to top the noodles and fish with sauce provençale (see p. 30) substituting chanterelles for *champignons de Paris*.

Ingredients

40 oz lotte
4 oz bread crumbs
4 oz canola oil
16 oz egg noodles
2 oz melted sweet butter
2 oz parsley or chives, chopped
saffron sauce (see p. 35)

OVEN ROASTED STEAK OF LOTTE (Monkfish) with Green Peppercorn Sauce

Ingredients

4 fillets of cleaned lotte, approximately 8 oz each, skinless, boneless and kept whole
1 oz green peppercorn along with its bottled liquid
1 tsp brandy
bread crumbs for coating
1 Tbsp oil for brushing
salt and pepper to taste
velouté sauce (see p. 14)

SERVES 4

Preheat oven to 450 F.

Pat dry lotte salt and pepper to taste.

Drain green peppercorns and reserve liquid for later use.

In a small pan briefly sauté the peppercorns until dry. Add brandy and flambé.

Reduce to dry again (this will enhance the flavor of the peppercorns). Reserve them.

Proceed to make the *velouté* sauce. Set aside aside in a hot place or keep on very low. Add the liquid from the peppercorns.

Coat lotte fillets with bread crumbs.

In a heavy pan (cast iron would be ideal) place the coated lotte. Brush fillets with oil to prevent sticking.

Place in hot oven. Cook for 15 minutes or until done. The fish should be opaque and soft. Place on serving plate and ladle some of the sauce over the lotte and sprinkle the green peppercorns on top.

TOURNEDOS OF LOTTE (Monkfish) with Chunks of Lobster and Lobster Butter

SERVES 4

Prepare lobster butter.

Pat lotte dry. Season with salt and pepper. Heat the butter in a heavy skillet.

Sauté the lotte until just golden, about 3 minutes per side. Add the chopped shallots evenly around the fish, and continue cooking for another 2 minutes, turning once more.

Pour in the Cognac and cook for one minute longer. Lift out the fish and place on warm serving plates and keep warm.

Add half of the heavy cream to the skillet and continue cooking and stirring until the liquid is reduced by half.

Add the remaining cream and continue cooking until the mixture is thick enough to cover the back of your spoon. Lower the heat and add the lobster butter 1 tsp at a time, whisking constantly.

Strain the sauce through a sieve into a clean pan and add the lobster meat. Simmer on low heat for two minutes.

Spoon lobster pieces onto serving plates between pieces of lotte. Top with sauce and serve immediately.

Ingredients

12 pieces of lotte fillet, skin off (about 2 oz each)
1/2 cup clarified butter
1/4 cup shallots, finely chopped
1/4 cup Cognac
2 cups heavy cream
1/2 cup lobster butter (see p. 24)
the meat from 2 1 1/4 lb lobsters, cut into thick slices
salt and pepper to taste
parsley for decoration

BAKED STUFFED
MACKEREL
with Mushrooms

Ingredients

1 dressed mackerel (about
    3 1/2 lb), split and
    thoroughly dry inside
    and out
1/2 tsp salt
ground black pepper
6 Tbsp (3/4 stick) sweet
    butter
1 small onion, minced
1 Tbsp fresh parsley,
    minced
1/4 lb mushrooms,
    coarsely chopped
1 cup soft bread crumbs
1 tsp fresh mint, minced
    (or dried mint may be
    used)
salt to taste
 ground black pepper to
    taste

SERVES 4

Preheat oven to 350 F.

Sprinkle mackerel inside and out with salt and pepper.

In a small heavy saucepan or skillet melt 3 Tbsp of the butter.

Stir in onion, parsley, and mushrooms, and sauté for about 5 minutes until onions are tender.

Add bread crumbs and mint and season with salt and pepper to taste
.

Mix well and stuff mackerel with the mixture.

Use poultry pins or toothpicks to keep fish closed.

Make 2 or 3 gashes in the skin.

Place fish in a lightly buttered shallow baking dish.

Dot with remaining 3 Tbsp butter.

Bake for about 50 minutes.

PAN-FRIED FILLET OF OMBLE CHEVALIER
with Brown Butter

SERVES 4

Make sure all bones are removed from fillets.

Dredge in flour, and shake off excess.

Add salt and pepper to taste.

In a heated sauté pan, add clarified butter and over high heat sauté fillets, skin side up, for about 2 to 3 minutes.

Turn fish once (skin side down) and continue to sauté for another 2 minutes, always at high heat.

Remove fish fillets from skillet onto a warm serving plate. Drain used clarified butter.

Put skillet back on the fire and add salted butter. Let sizzle until golden brown.

Squeeze lemon into pan and pour mixture over fish and serve at once.

Garnish with 2 steamed potatoes or one potato and a green vegetable.

Ingredients

4 fillets omble chevalier, boneless
salt and pepper
2 oz clarified butter or vegetable oil
2 Tbsp salted butter
flour for dredging
1 lemon

BAKED OMBLE CHEVALIER
with Port, Sherry, &
Julienned Fresh Vegetables

Ingredients

4 1 lb omble chevalier,
  cleaned and boneless
1 carrot, peeled and
  julienned
1 leek julienned
1/4 lb snow peas,
  julienned
1 stalk celery, julienned
1 cup dry Sherry
1 cup dry vermouth

1 cup white wine cream
  sauce (see p. 33)
1/2 cup Port

SERVES 4

Preheat oven to 400 F.

Poach all vegetables and stuff inside fish.

Place omble chevalier in baking dish and top with Sherry and vermouth.

Bake for 15–17 minutes at 400 F.

Make white wine sauce (see p. 33).

To make port wine sauce, reduce Port wine by half and cook 10 minutes over low heat.

Add Port wine to white wine sauce and cook for 10 minutes over low heat.

Remove fish to platter and serve with Port wine sauce on top.

BROILED FILLET OF YELLOW PIKE
with Bouquetiere of Vegetables

SERVES 4

Coat pike fillets with bread crumbs.

Sauté over medium heat in canola oil for 10 minutes or until done. Turn once.

Serve with freshly steamed vegetables of your choice.

Ingredients

4 10 oz yellow pike fillets, cleaned
4 oz bread crumbs
2 oz canola oil
assorted vegetables to taste

POLLOCK PARMESAN

Ingredients

4 pollock fillets
  (about 2 lb), or haddock,
  cod, whiting, etc.
  may be used instead
1/3 cup flour
2 eggs, beaten
3/4 cup fine bread crumbs
1/4 cup Parmesan cheese,
  grated
pinch of paprika
1 tsp salt
generous sprinkling of
  ground white pepper
l/2 tsp oregano
1 Tbsp fresh parsley, minced
dash of cayenne
6 Tbsp (3/4 stick) sweet
  butter
1 Tbsp corn oil
8 oz tomato sauce
  (see p. 40)

SERVES 4

Prepare tomato sauce, or reheat 8 oz from your favorite refrigerated supply.

Dust fillets with flour and dip well in beaten eggs.

Thoroughly mix bread crumbs, grated cheese, paprika, salt, pepper, oregano, parsley, and cayenne.

Dip fish in the seasoned crumbs, coating thoroughly.

Heat butter and oil in a large heavy skillet until frothy but not brown.It is best to use a non-stick pan.

Fry fish until golden brown and crispy for about 5 minutes on one side.

Turn carefully with tongs and brown on the other side until crispy, about 4 or 5 minutes.

Drain fish fillets on a paper towel.

Tomato sauce may be spooned over the fish before serving.

FILLET OF POMPANO
with Rum Raisins

SERVES 4

Rinse fillets and pat dry.

Salt each fillet lightly, dredge in flour and shake off excess.

Sauté in clarified butter over medium-high heat until crusty and lightly golden, about 2–3 minutes per side.

Transfer to warm serving plates (2 fillets per serving).

In a saucepan, melt the 4 Tbsp of whole butter with the raisins and rum.

Bring the mixture to a slow boil over medium-high heat. Continue bubbling for 2 more minutes, allowing the sauce to reduce and thicken.

Spoon the sauce over each fillet of fish in equal amounts.

Ingredients

8 fillets of Pompano,
    4 to 6 oz each
1/2 cup flour
4 Tbsp (1/2 stick) clarified
    butter for sautéing
4 Tbsp (1/2 stick) butter
1/2 cup raisins
1/2 cup dark Meyer's rum

POMPANO FILLETS
en Papillote

Ingredients

4 pompano fillets (about
  2 lb)
4 heart-shaped pieces of
  cooking parchment,
  large enough to wrap
  each fillet
4 Tbsp (1/2 stick) sweet
  butter
1 1/2–2 Tbsp flour
1 tsp salt
pinch of cayenne
dash of ground white
  pepper
1 cup half-and-half
1/4 lb mushrooms, finely
  chopped
1 small onion, finely
  chopped
1 shallot, minced
1 Tbsp fresh parsley,
  minced
salt to taste
 ground white pepper to
  taste

SERVES 4

Preheat oven to 425 F. Place each fillet on half of the
"heart" of parchment paper.

Melt 2 Tbsp of the butter in the top part of a double
boiler over boiling water.

Blend in flour, salt, cayenne, and white pepper, stirring
constantly until smooth. Gradually add half-and-half
and continue stirring until sauce begins to thicken.
Remove from heat and keep warm over the hot water.

Melt remaining 2 Tbsp butter in a small heavy skillet.
Sauté mushrooms, onion, and shallot in butter for
about 2 or 3 minutes.

Top each pompano fillet with cream sauce and the
mushroom mixture. Sprinkle with parsley and season
with salt and pepper to taste.

Fold the parchment paper across the top of the fish
and sauce and crimp the edges securely, sealing all
the way around.

Place the parchment-covered fish on a preheated
cookie sheet in the oven, and bake until the parchment
is puffed up and browned, about 15 minutes.

Serve in the parchment pouch on preheated plates.

STEAMED RAY (Skate) FILLET
with Tarragon and Capers

SERVES 4

Dip ray in clarified butter and tarragon vinegar and steam for 5–6 minutes.

Place on plate and top with fresh tarragon, capers, and browned butter.

Ingredients

- 4 2–3 lb ray wings, filleted and skinned
- 4 oz clarified butter
- 8 oz tarragon vinegar
- 4 sprigs fresh tarragon
- 4 oz capers
- 4 oz browned butter

SAUTÉED ROUGET BARBET
with Rosemary Beurre Blanc

Ingredients

8 rouget fillets, skin on
      (2 per person)
salt and pepper
2 Tbsp flour
2 Tbsp clarified butter
2 oz fresh rosemary
      (reserve 2 sprigs for
      decoration)
beurre blanc (see p. 7)

SERVES 4

Make *beurre blanc*, stirring in all but two sprigs of rosemary. Set aside in warm place for later use.

Pat fish dry.

Season with salt and pepper.

Dredge in flour. Shake off excess.

Preheat sauté pan. Add clarified butter.

Sauté fish over medium high heat, skin-side first, and continue to cook over medium heat for another 2—3 minutes. Turn once and cook 2—3 minutes more. Fish should be opaque and firm.

Remove from heat, drain and place on warm platter.

Ladle *beurre blanc* to cover plates in a thin layer. VERY CAREFULLY, with a spatula (rouget barbet breaks easily), place fillets, skinside up, in a "V" shape, onto plates, with the small ends of each fish touching the other.

Place 1/2 sprig of rosemary over fillet for the garnish.

Serve with steamed *haricots vert* and boiled potatoes.

BROILED SALMON
FILLET
with Cucumber Hollandaise

SERVES 4

Preheat broiler.

Brush fillets with butter or oil. Sprinkle with bread crumbs.

Place broiling rack with fish under the broiler (flame should be at least 6 inches away from fish). Baste or brush with butter or oil if you think it is necessary in order to avoid drying out the fish.

Broil for about 5 to 6 minutes, turn once and continue to cook for another 5 minutes. Make sure not to char salmon skin. Serve at once with cucumber Hollandaise on the side.

TO MAKE CUCUMBER HOLLANDAISE

Prepare Hollandaise (see p. 20) and set aside, keeping it warm, over the steamy hot water of a double boiler.

Peel cucumbers and slice in half and remove seeds with a spoon. In food processor or by hand, chop very fine and drain well. (The best method is to squeeze cucumber in a cloth napkin until all liquid is removed). Set aside.

Chop fresh dill very fine, mix with cucumber and gradually incorporate into the Hollandaise.

Ingredients

4 fillets of salmon
2 oz bread crumbs
2 oz clarified butter or
    vegetable oil
2 small cucumbers
2 sprigs fresh dill
salt and pepper to taste
Hollandaise sauce
    (see p. 20)

POACHED FILLET OF SALMON
in Champagne Sauce with Salmon Caviar

Ingredients

4 boneless fillets of salmon
2 oz salmon caviar
4 Tbsp (1/2 stick) butter
2 Tbsp flour
2 cups white wine
salt and pepper to taste
1 cup Champagne sauce
(see p. 8)

SERVES 4

TO POACH SALMON

In enamel or stainless steel sauté pan or skillet put white wine.

Add fish and season to taste.

Simmer over low heat for approximately 8 minutes.

Spoon Champagne sauce to form a thin coating on the serving plate (make sure there are no lumps).

Place poached salmon in the center of plate, and with a small spoon, garnish the caviar all around the inside edge of the plate.

Serve immediately. Some suggested accompaniments are steamed white potatoes and sautéed *haricots verts*.

ESCALOPE OF SALMON
in White Wine
Cream Sauce with Sorrel

SERVES 4

Slice salmon into thin escalopes.

Place escalopes between wax paper sheets and, with a meat mallet, pound them, making sure not to tear them apart. Refrigerate.

Prepare white wine cream sauce. Set aside in warm place.

Preheat a sauté pan. Dredge fish with flour very lightly, and shake off any excess.

Sauté the salmon escalopes over high flame for about 1–2 minutes. Season to taste with salt and pepper, and drain on paper towel.

Cover tips of escallopes with white wine cream sauce.

NOTE
Clean the fresh sorrel leaves by pulling out the stems. Garnish with very rthinly sliced leaves, bunch them together into a chiffonad, (shaping them like a cigar).

Serve immediately.

Ingredients

32 oz salmon (center cut)
salt and pepper to taste
1/2 cup all-purpose flour
white wine cream sauce
    (see p. 32)
1 oz fresh sorrel

SEARED FILLET OF NORTH ATLANTIC SALMON
in a Horseradish Crust with Shallot Beurre Blanc

Ingredients

4 fillets of Atlantic salmon (skinned and boned)
3 slices white bread, toasted
1 small fresh horseradish root,(peeled
8 Tbsp (1 stick) butter at room temperature
1 oz smoked salmon
1 Tbsp parsley, chopped
2 oz clarified butter
1 Tbsp fresh chives, choppe)
beurre blanc (see p. 7)
4 shallots

SERVES 4

Prepare *beurre blanc*, mix in shallots and set aside for later use.

Toast bread. In food processor, grate toasted bread into coarse crumbs.

Peel fresh horseradish and finely grate it in the food processor. In same food processor bowl, mix in bread crumbs, horseradish, smolked salmon, and chopped parsley.

Gradually add butter, using pulsating speed, blending well, until the consistency of the mixture is a paste.

Spread paste between two sheets of waxed paper and, with a meat tenderizer, meat mallet or rolling pin, pound to a very thin sheet.

Cut sheet into individual shapes corresponding to the shape of the fillet, pile on top of one another, and place in the refrigerator.

Preheat a thick skillet over high heat.

Add clarified butterand sear salmon fillets on both sides.

Cook on each side for approximately 5 minutes, being sure to turn fish to avoid burning or drying the outside of the fish.

Drain and set aside. Preheat broiler. Get the crust from the refrigerator, removepaper sheets from crust, and place one on top of each fillet.

 Place fish fillets under broiler for a few seconds, until the crust turns to a light toast color. In a serving plate, spoon enough *beurre blanc* to cover plate with a thin layer.

Place fish on top of sauce.

Garnish with chopped fresh chives.

POACHED FILLET OF SALMON
in White Wine Beurre Blanc with Pink Peppercorns

Ingredients

4 fillets salmon
3/4 oz pink peppercorns
1 cup white wine
2 cups fish stock
   (see p. 48)
beurre blanc (see p. 7)
salt and pepper to taste

SERVES 4

Prepare *beurre blanc* and add pink peppercorns. For a stronger flavor, crack peppercorns before adding to reduction. Set *beurre blanc* in warm place.

TO POACH THE SALMON

Pour white wine and fish stock into a large saucepan.

Bring almost to a boil, add fish, and reduce heat.

Simmer over low heat for 8 minutes, turning fish once.

After simmering, remove skin from the fillets.

On a warm serving plate, spoon enough *beurre blanc* to cover the bottom of the plate thinly.

Place fish on sauce, adding some of the remaining pink peppercorns for garnish.

Serve immediately while it is hot.

Suggested accompaniment: steamed white potato and a sautéed or steamed green vegetable.

BROILED RED SNAPPER
with Sauce Maltaise

SERVES 4

Make sauce Maltaise.

Season fillets with bread crumbs, salt and pepper.

Put on broiling rack rubbed with canola oil and cook for 5–6 minutes or until done.

Serve with Maltaise sauce on the side and sections of blood orange and blanched zest used in the sauce Maltaise recipe.

Ingredients

4 10 oz red snapper fillets
4 oz bread crumbs
salt and pepper to taste
2 oz canola oil
sauce Maltaise (see p. 22)

POACHED KING SALMON
with Cucumber Salad

Ingredients

2–3 cucumbers, peeled
    and thinly sliced
1 cup Oyster Bar House
    Dressing (see p. 28) or
    white vinegar may be
    used
3 qt water
4 whole black peppercorns
1 bay leaf
1 large onion, finely
    chopped
1 large carrot, finely
    chopped
1 large stalk celery, finely
    chopped
4 sprigs of fresh parsley
1 cup dry white wine
1 Tbsp salt

SERVES 12 TO 16. ALLOW 1/2 POUND PER PERSON

Marinate peeled and thinly sliced cucumbers in the
Oyster Bar House Dressing orin a small amount of
plain white vinegar in the refrigerator for 2 or 3 hours
until salmon is ready to serve.

Bring water to a boil in a large heavy kettle or
saucepan.

Add peppercorns, bay leaf, onion, carrot, celery,
parsley, wine, and salt.

Boil for about 15 minutes. Reduce heat and simmer for
about 1 1/2 or 2 hours.

Remove from heat, strain, and set bouillon aside to
cool.

Discard the vegetables.

Pour the cooled bouillon into a fish poacher or an
oblong pan large enough to hold the salmon.

Rinse the salmon and wrap it loosely in a piece of
cheesecloth. Leave the ends of the cheesecloth free
and long enough so you can lift the fish in and out of
the poacher or pan.

Lift the salmon into the bouillon and bring just to a boil.

Reduce heat and simmer over low heat for about 6 to 8 minutes for each lb of fish. The internal temperature reading should be 140 degrees.

Keep the cheesecloth well soaked with the bouillon while the fish simmers.

When the salmon is cooked, remove it immediately to a large serving platter. Set the bouillon aside for another use. Unwrap and discard the cheesecloth.

While the fish is cooling, carefully remove its skin and any fatty gray sections with a sharp knife until only the pink flesh remains.

Pat the platter around the salmon dry with a paper towel to remove any excess liquid.

Drain and arrange the cucumbers attractively around the fish. Arrange thin lemon slices on top of the salmon.

Garnish the cucumbers with cherry tomatoes and parsley sprigs.

Ingredients (Cont'd)

whole king or Chinook salmon (about 6-8 lb), dressed, or with the head and tail on
3–4 lemons, thinly sliced
24–32 cherry tomatoes
bunch of fresh parsley sprigs

SALMON STEAKS
TERIYAKI

Ingredients

4 salmon steaks
(about 2 lb)

FOR THE MARINADE

3/4 cup soy sauce
1/2 cup brown sugar
1/4 cup rice wine (sake)
3/4 cup water
1 Tbsp gingerminced
1 tsp dry basil
1 tsp garlic, minced
1 Tbsp sesame oil

SERVES 4

Preheat broiler for about 10 minutes.

Combine all the ingredients in a bowl large enough to contyain all the salmon steaks and mix well.

Marinate salmon steaks for about 1 hour.

Broil fish on one side for about 4 minutes or until nicely browned. Baste several times with the marinade while broiling.

Turn salmon carefully with tongs and broil on the other side for about 5 or 6 minutes, basting several times, until nicely browned.

Heat leftover marinade and drizzle over salmon before serving.

SAUTÉED BONELESS SALMON FILLETS
with Almond Beurre Blanc

SERVES 4

Lightly flour salmon fillets.

In a large frying pan, add oil and sauté fillets for 4 minutes on each side.

MAKE ALMOND *BEURRE BLANC*

Add to *beurre blanc* Amaretto liqueur and almond paste. Mix in smoothly.

Serve salmon fillets with 2 oz of almond *beurre blanc* poured on top and garnished with sliced almonds

Ingredients

4 10–12 oz boneless baby
   steelhead salmon fillets
4 oz flour
2 oz canola oil
8 oz *beurre blanc*
   (see p. 11)
2 oz almond paste
2 oz Amaretto liqueur
1 oz almonds, toasted and
   thinly sliced

BOSTON SCROD
with Lemon Butter

Ingredients

4 scrod fillets (about 2 lb)
8 Tbsp (1 stick) sweet
    butter
2 Tbsp fresh lemon juice
1 tsp salt
generous sprinkling of
    ground white pepper
1 Tbsp fresh parsley,
    minced
2 Tbsp fine bread crumbs

SERVES 4

Preheat the broiler for about 10 minutes.

Melt butter in a small heavy saucepan over low heat.

Add lemon juice, salt, pepper, and parsley.

Arrange scrod fillets in one layer in a shallow baking dish.

Pour lemon butter over all, coating thoroughly.

Broil fish for about 5 minutes, basting several times with lemon butter sauce.

Sprinkle bread crumbs over the fish and broil for 5 more minutes, or until the scrod flakes easily with a fork.

Spoon lemon butter over fillets before serving.

SCROD STEAMED IN BAMBOO
with Garden Vegetables

SERVES 4

In bamboo steamer, arrange sliced potatoes over a bed of spinach.

Place scrod on top of potatoes and sliced carrots on top of scrod.

Steam for approximately 12 minutes.

Place butter and capers in saucepan and heat for 1 minute.

Pour butter and capers over fish and garnish with lemon.

Ingredients

4 10 oz portions of scrod
2 large baking potatoes, peeled and sliced
1/2 lb spinach
3 thinly sliced medium carrots
3 oz capers
1/4 lb sweet butter, browned
2 large lemons, sectioned

BROILED SHAD ROE
with Bacon on Toast Points

Ingredients

4 shad roe
2 Tbsp (1/4 stick) sweet
    butter, melted
4 slices hot toast
4 slices bacon, broiled or
    fried crisp
8 sprigs of watercress
4 lemon wedges

SERVES 4

Preheat broiler for about 10 minutes.

Brush roe with melted butter and place under the broiler until golden brown but not crusty. Turn gently and broil till firm.

Serve on hot toast.

Garnish with strips of bacon, sprigs of watercress, and wedges of lemon.

BROILED SHAD
AND SHAD ROE
with Bacon and Tomato

SERVES 4

Preheat oven to 550 F.

Slice the tomatoes in half and discard the insides. Set aside the halves.

Sprinkle 1 oz of the bread crumbs over shad and shad roe.

Mix remaining bread crumbs with clarified butter, chopped garlic, and parsley.

Spoon mixture onto tomato halves. Bake until soft, about 15 minutes. Remove from oven and keep warm.

Preheat broiler. Place fillets and roe on oiled broiling rack. Broil the shad and the shad roe for 3 minutes.

Turn the shad roe only and add the tomatoes.

Continue to broil for another 2 minutes. Make sure not to over cook either the fillet or the roe. Do not burn the tomatoes.

Arrange one each of the fillet, roe, and tomatoes, along with boiled potatoes, on warm serving plates.

Garnish with strips of crisp bacon placed diagonally over the fillet and roe.

Ingredients

4 half shad fillets (approximately 5 oz each)
4 half shad roe (approximately 5 oz each)
2 medium size tomatoes
3 oz bread crumbs
1 tsp chopped garlic
2 oz fresh chopped parsley
2 oz clarified sweet butter
8 crisply cooked bacon strips
boiled potatoes

MAKO SHARK STEAK
au Poivre

Ingredients

8 thick slices mako shark
    (about 10 oz each),
    skin removed
salt
1/4 cup coarsely crushed
    black pepper
1/2 cup clarified sweet
    butter
3 tsp chopped shallot
1/3 cup Cognac, plus
    more as needed
2 cups heavy cream
2 Tbsp veal demi-glace or
    1/3 cup veal stock
    (see pp. 42-43)

SERVES 8

Pat shark slices dry and salt lightly.

Arrange crushed pepper on a large plate or sheet of waxed paper and dredge each slice of fish in pepper, shaking off excess to leave a light coating.

Heat clarified butter in large heavy skillet until hot.

Working in batches if necessary, sauté fish slices until crusty and lightly golden, 2 to 3 minutes per side.

Transfer to warm serving plates.

Pour off all but 1 Tbsp butter from skillet. Add shallots and toss briefly.

CAREFULLY add 1/3 cup Cognac to avoid excess flaming. Add cream, veal demi-glace and any juices from the fish.

Boil until reduced to consistency that will lightly coat the back of a spoon.

Adjust seasoning with salt, and a few drops of Cognac.

Strain through a fine sieve over fish and serve.

ESCALLOPES OF MAKO SHARK FILLET
with Lemon and Caper

SERVES 8

Make the piccata sauce.

Dredge the shark escallopes lightly with flour. Pat to remove excess.

Heat clarified butter to sizzling. Put shark escallopes into pan.

Sauté, in batches if necessary, for 1 1/2 minutes on each side, until lightly browned.

Remove from pan and place on warm plates.

Wipe sauté pan clean. Combine the butter, lemon, and capers.

Stirring constantly, cook briefly until butter turns lightly brown.

Add white wine and cook for another 30 seconds.

Pour sauce over the fish, and garnish with a sprig of fresh parsley.

Ingredients

- 8 10 oz fillets of mako shark, sliced into thin escallopes
- 1/4 cup flour
- 3 Tbsp sweet clarified butter
- 2 lemons
- 4 oz capers
- 6 oz white wine
- sprig of fresh parsley
- piccata sauce (see p. 29)

GRILLED
EXTRA LARGE SMELTS

Ingredients

4 lb Canadian smelts,
   cleaned
2 oz bread crumbs
salt and pepper
2 oz olive oil
8 oz Tartar sauce
   (see p. 39)

SERVES 6-8

Season smelts with bread crumbs, salt and pepper.

Rub a small amount of oil on the smelts and grill for 3 minutes on each side.

Serve with Tartar sauce.

SMELTS
with Caper Sauce

SERVES 4

Dip smelts in cream.

Thoroughly blend flour, cornmeal, salt, pepper, and paprika.

Roll smelts in this mixture until evenly coated.

Heat oil in a large heavy skillet until just sizzling.

Fry smelts for 2–3 minutes on each side, or until nicely browned. Turn with a slotted spoon.

Meanwhile, melt butter, lemon juice, capers, and parsley in a small saucepan.

Remove smelts with a slotted spoon to a paper towel to drain.

Place on heated serving plates and pour caper sauce over the fish to serve.

Ingredients

2 lb smelts
1/2 cup light cream
1/3 cup flour
1/3 cup cornmeal
2 tsp salt
dash of ground black
    pepper
pinch of paprika
1 cup corn oil
4 Tbsp (1/2 stick) sweet
    butter
1 tsp fresh lemon juice
1 Tbsp capers
1 Tbsp fresh parsley,
    minced

PAN-FRIED PINK SNAPPER
with
Lemongrass Beurre Blanc

Ingredients

4 pink snapper fillets
   (skin on)
2 Tbsp flour
salt and pepper
2 Tbsp clarified sweet
   butter
1/2 lb fresh peeled lemon
   grass, with the center
   sliced all the way
   through
beurre blanc (see p. 11)
lemongrass

SERVES 4

While cooking the *beurre blanc*, add 2/3 of the fresh lemon grass center, coarsely chopped or minced.

Pat fillets dry, dredge in flour, shake off excess.

Season with salt and pepper.

Preheat sauté pan over medium high heat and add clarified butter.

Place fillet skin side up in sauté pan.

Cook fish for about three minutes, if necessary, in batches, keeping previous batches in a warm place.

Turn (skin side down now). Continue to cook for two more minutes.

When fish is ready, drain and place on serving plates. Spoon sauce over fish. Garnish with very thinly sliced lemongrass.

Serve immediately.

NOTE
For best flavor and fragrance briefly steam the lemongrass before using as a garnish.

POACHED YELLOWTAIL SNAPPER with Citrus Beurre Blanc

SERVES 4

Peel, julienne and poach the zest from all 4 fruits. Reserve for later use.

Section and save the flesh of all 4 fruits for the *beurre blanc.*

In an oven-proof glass dish or deep metal baking pan put parsley, chopped shallots and *fish stock*

Submerge fish in the liquid and cook over medium heat for about 5-6 minutes.

Fish should be flaky and opaque.

Make *beurre blanc,* and while cooking add the reserved flesh of the four fruits.

When fish is ready, very carefully, using a wide spatula, place fillets onto serving plates.

Spoon sauce on top of fillet and decorate with the mixed zest of all four fruits.

Serve at once with steamed asparagus spears, fresh baby carrots and boiled potatoes.

Ingredients

8 yellowtail fillets, skin on
    (serving 2 fillets per
    person)
1 lemon
1 orange
1 lime
1 grapefruit
2 fresh shallots (chopped)
2 sprigs fresh parsley
1 qt *fish stock*
    (see p. 48)
beurre blanc (see p. 7)
 salt and pepper

FILLET OF SOLE BONNE FEMME

Ingredients

4 fillets of sole
4 Tbsp (1/2 stick) sweet
 butter
2 shallots, finely chopped
1/4 lb mushrooms with
 stems, thinly sliced or
 coarsely chopped
1 Tbsp fresh parsley,
 minced
3/4 cup dry white wine
salt to taste
dash of ground white
 pepper
1 tsp fresh lemon juice
8 sprigs of parsley

Heat butter in a large heavy skillet, but don't brown. Add the shallots, half the mushrooms, and the fish.

Cover the fish with the rest of the mushrooms and the minced parsley.

Pour in the wine, and add salt and pepper.

Turn up heat to not quite boiling and cook for 3–4 minutes, basting constantly.

Remove fish to warm serving dishes with a slotted spoon.

Add lemon juice and cook the mushroom and wine sauce for about 1 minute.

Pour over the fillets before serving, and garnish with fresh sprigs of parsley.

PAN FRIED DOVER SOLE

SERVES 4

Dredge sole in flour, shake off excess, and add salt and pepper to taste.

To a preheated skillet or sauté pan, add clarified butter. Sauté the sole over high heat for about 5 minutes.

When fish is golden brown, turn once, and continue sauté for another 3 to 4 minutes.

Check fish for doneness by inserting spatula or spoon under the backbone of the fish and prying upwards so that the flesh separates from bones. If it separates, it is done.

Transfer fish to warm serving plates.

In same sauté pan, add butter. Let sizzle until brown, squeeze in lemon and mix well. Pour over fish.

Serve hot at once. Garnish each plate with a half or quartered lemon, and fresh parsley.

Ingredients

4 Dover sole (skinned and
   cut from the center)
flour
salt and pepper to taste
3 oz clarified butter or oil
2 Tbsp butter, salted
2 lemons
2 or 3 sprigs fresh parsley,
   chopped

GOUJONETTES OF LEMON SOLE

Ingredients

4 fillets of lemon sole,
    approximately 8 to 10
    oz each
salt and pepper to taste
2 cups flour
2 eggs, beaten
2 cups bread crumbs
2 cups canola or peanut
    oil
1 lemon
sprig of fresh parsley

SERVES 4

Pat each fillet dry. Sprinkle with salt and pepper.

Cut the fillets into strips about 1 inch wide.

Have three soup plates ready: one with the flour, a second with the beaten eggs, and the third with bread crumbs.

Dredge each strip first in the flour, then dip into the egg mixture, and, finally, coat with bread crumbs.

Heat the oil in a deep frying pan to 375 F.

Add fish strips.

When the goujonettes turn golden brown (2 to 3 minutes), remove from the oil, and drain them on paper towels.

Serve while they are hot, with a sprig of parsley and a wedge of lemon.

POACHED LEMON SOLE
with Mussels and Shrimp

SERVES 8

In a medium-sized, covered sauce pan, steam open black mussels. Drain and reserve liquid.

In same covered saucepan, add liquid and cook shrimp for about 2–3 minutes only.

Let shrimp cool in the cooking liquid. Peel and devein them.

Remove mussels from the shell and discard shell.

Place together mussels and cleaned deveined shrimp. Keep in a warm place for future use.

In a shallow pan, top sole with stock.

Poach in simmering *court bouillion* for about 5 minutes. Sole will turn opaque, turn lighter in color, and become soft to the touch.

Remove sole from liquid and set on serving platter or individual dishes. Top with mussels and shrimp.

Spoon some *sauce velouté* to cover. Spoon over some mousseline sauce and gratiné until golden.

Serve immediately. Suggested accompaniment: boiled potatoes.

Ingredients

8 fillets of lemon sole
16 black saltwater mussels
    (4 each, but get extra
    in case some will not
    open)

12 medium shrimp (3 for
    each serving)
8 oz fish stock (see p. 48)
mousseline sauce
    (see p. 27)
sauce velouté (see p. 14)

FRIED BABY SQUID
with Mustard Fruit Mayonnaise

Ingredients

4 lb baby squid, cleaned
2 cups tempura flour (rice flour)
1 egg, beaten
1 cup mayonnaise (see p. 23)
1/2 cup imported Italian mustard fruit, pitted and chopped
1/2 tsp nutmeg
1 Tbsp Cognac

SERVES 4

Dry squid, then add beaten egg and flour; mix well.

Deep fry for 1 minute on high heat.

Make mustard fruit mayonnaise by mixing mayonnaise, mustard fruit, nutmeg, and Cognac.

Spoon evenly over squid and serve immediately.

ST. PIERRE
with Barolo Sauce

SERVES 4

Barolo sauce. (See red wine cream sauce p.33).
Wherever red wine is called for, substitute Barolo.

Keep sauce in a warm place.

Make mousseline sauce. Keep sauce in a warm place.

Pat fish dry. Salt and pepper to taste.

Dredge fillets in flour, shaking off any excess.

Preheat sauté pan. Add clarified butter.

Sauté fish for about 4 minutes each side, until golden
brown.

When fish is done, drain and set aside.

Spoon Barolo sauce onto four warm serving plates.
Carefully place each fillet on a plate. Then spread
mousseline sauce over each fillet (only over the fish).
Sprinkle chopped tarragon leaves over the mousseline
sauce.

Serve small peeled boiled potatoes with this dish.

Ingredients

4 St. Pierre fillets (skinned)
salt and pepper
2 Tbsp flour
2 Tbsp clarified butter
Barolo sauce (see recipe
    for red wine cream
    sauce p. 32)
mousseline sauce
    (see p. 27)
4 sprigs chopped, fresh
    tarragon—leaves only

POACHED ST. PIERRE
Champignons
de Paris Provençale

Ingredients

4 St. Pierre fillets
1 cup fish *velouté*
   (see p. 14)*sauce*
   Provençale
   (see p. 30)
1 cup small white
   mushrooms, sliced thin
2 Tbsp butter
1 qt *fish stock* for
   poaching plus 1/2 cup
   for the sauce
   (see p. 48)

SERVES 4

Make fish *velouté*. Set sauce in a warm place for future use.

Make *sauce Provençale*.

Sauté white mushrooms in butter. Add to *sauce Provençale*.

Set over low heat. Cook for10 minutes.

The *velouté* and *champignons de Paris* and *Provençale* sauces will now be ready for use.

In the quart of *court bouillon* proceed to poach fillets. Use an oven-proof glass dish or deep metal baking pan. Submerge fish in the liquid and cook over medium heat for about 10 to12 minutes.

Test for doneness. Fish should be flaky and opaque.

When fish is ready, place on the serving dish and, taking care not to cover the St. Pierre too deeply, top with *velouté* sauce, and top off the sauce by spooning on *sauce Provençale*.

Serve at once.

BROILED LAKE STURGEON
with Anchovy Butter

SERVES 4

Season sturgeon with bread crumbs and oil.

Grill for 6–7 minutes on each side.

Make anchovy butter.

Place 1 Tbsp of anchovy butter on top of sturgeon and place under broiler until melted.

Ingredients

4 10 oz portions of
   sturgeon
4 oz bread crumbs
2 oz canola oil
anchovy butter (see p. 4)

ESCALLOP OF STURGEON STROGANOFF

Ingredients

8 4oz slices of sturgeon
1/4 cup flour
1/4 cup canola oil
6 oz mushrooms
Stroganoff sauce
    (see p. 37)
demi-glace
 (see pp. 42-43)
2 Tbsp sour cream

SERVES 4

Make Stroganoff sauce.

Lightly flour and sauté sturgeon over low heat in canola oil.

Remove sturgeon from pan, add mushrooms, and sauté for 2 minutes.

Add Stroganoff sauce.

Add 2 Tbsp sour cream and bring to a light simmer.

Put sturgeon back in pan containing the sauce and cook for an additional minute.

Place 2 pieces of sturgeon on each plate and pour 2 Tbsp of Stroganoff sauce on top of each piece.

LAKE STURGEON TONNATO
with Cucumber Salad

SERVES 6-8

Make slits in sturgeon fillets.

Place 2 garlic cloves and 2 anchovy fillets within.

Poach in chicken stock for 20 minutes.

Cool and slice thin, wide slices to cover entire plate.

Make tonnato sauce.

Top with 12 oz tonnato sauce and sprinkle capers over sauce.

Garnish with lemon and lime slices and cucumber salad on side.

TO MAKE CUCUMBER SALAD

Mix cucumbers, Spanish onion, dill, white vinegar, salt and white pepper and sugar.

Ingredients

41 lb sturgeon fillets, boneless
8 garlic cloves, whole
8 small anchovy fillets, whole

4 cups chicken broth
2 Tbsp capers
1 lemon, sliced
1 lime sliced
2 large cucumbers, peeled, seeded, and sliced
1/2 Spanish onion, sliced
2 Tbsp dill, chopped

2 Tbsp white vinegar
salt and white pepper to taste
2 Tbsp sugar
tonnato sauce (see p. 41)

PANFRIED LAKE STURGEON FILLET
with Wild Mushrooms

Ingredients

4 8–10 oz sturgeon fillets
2 oz flour
2 oz canola oil
1 oz shallots, chopped
1/4 Tbsp garlic, chopped
2 oz Shiitake mushrooms, stems removed, and sliced
2 oz Portobello mushrooms, stems removed, and sliced
2 oz chanterelle mushrooms, stems removed, and sliced
2 oz oyster mushrooms, stems removed, and sliced
1 1/4 cup demi-glace (see pp. 42-43)

SERVES 4

Lightly flour sturgeon fillets and pan fry in canola oil for 12–15 minutes.

Remove from pan and drain excess oil.

Add garlic and shallots and sauté for 1 minute.

Add all the mushrooms and sauté until brown.

Add demi-glace and reduce by half.

Add cooked sturgeon fillet and heat for 1 minute.

Serve with mushrooms and sauce on top of fillets.

SWORDFISH AMANDINE

SERVES 4

Cover broiler pan with aluminum foil and preheat for about 10 minutes.

Brown almonds in 2 Tbsp of the butter in a small skillet. Set aside and keep warm.

Melt remaining butter (6 Tbsp) in a small saucepan and add parsley and lemon juice.

Put swordfish on the broiler pan and pour 1 Tbsp Sherry over each steak.

Sprinkle with ground black pepper.

Spoon the butter mixture over each steak and broil on one side for about 8 minutes, basting constantly with the butter-Sherry mixture.

Turn fish carefully and broil on the other side for about 3–4 minutes until nicely browned, basting constantly.

Sprinkle shallots, paprika, and crisp crumbled bacon on the swordfish. Top with almonds before serving.

NOTE
Mako shark steaks may be used instead of swordfish.

Ingredients

4 swordfish steaks (about 2 lb)
1/2 cup blanched almonds, thinly sliced
8 Tbsp butter (1 stick), divided
1 Tbsp fresh parsley, minced
1 tsp fresh lemon juice
4 Tbsp Sherry
dash of ground black pepper
2 shallots, finely chopped (or green onions may be used)
paprika
4 slices bacon, broiled or fried crisp, and crumbled

BROCHETTE OF SWORDFISH
with Scallops, Mushrooms and Tomatoes

Ingredients

12 2oz swordfish cubes
  without skin
12 large sea scallops
8 large mushroom caps
8 large cherry tomatoes
1–2 cups white rice

MARINADE

1 Tbsp chopped shallots
2 Tbsp chopped garlic
1/2 cup lemon juice
1/2 cup lime juice
1 cup canola oil

SERVES 4

Combine ingredients for the marinade.

Arrange alternately 3 pieces each of swordfish and scallops, 2 mushroom caps, and 2 cherry tomatoes on each metal skewer.

Pour marinade over skewer and let sit for 1 hour.

Grill skewers for 4 minutes on each side.

Place on top of white rice and serve.

BLACKENED SPICY SWORDFISH FILLETS
with Polenta

SERVES 4

TO MAKE POLENTA
Boil water in heavy cast iron saucepan.
Gradually whisk in cornmeal. Add Shiitake
mushrooms. Continue whisking until mixture boils and
begins to thicken, about 2 minutes.

Reduce heat and cook cornmeal for about 30 minutes
until thick, whisking occasionally with wooden spoon
or thick stiff whip (polenta can be prepared 2 to 4
hours ahead).

Transfer polenta to a baking sheet and refrigerate.
When needed, polenta should be reheated either by
sautéing, baking or simply steaming. If sautéing or
baking, add canola oil to bottom of sauté pan.

Mix together well all blackening spices. Have a cast
iron pan very hot.

Dredge fish fillets in spices, dip into clarified butter and
carefully place on hot skillet. Cook on first side for
about 3 to 4 minutes. You will see fish turning opaque.

Turn and continue to cook for another 3 to 4 minutes.

Cut fillets in half. Serve very hot with polenta squares,
diamonds or rounds (use cookie cutters for different
shapes).

Ingredients

4 5 oz swordfish fillets
     (about 3/4 in thick)
3 oz clarified butter

BLACKENING SPICES

1 Tbsp paprika
2 1/2 tsp salt
1 tsp onion powder
I tsp cayenne pepper
1/4 tsp white pepper
3/4 tsp black pepper
1/2 tsp thyme
1/2 tsp oregano

POLENTA

4 cups water
1 cup cornmeal
10 Shiitake mushrooms,
     sliced thin
1/2 cup canola oil

CHARCOAL-GRILLED MARINATED SWORDFISH

Ingredients

4 10-oz swordfish steaks, about 1 in thick

MARINADE

3/4 cup olive oil
1 tsp salt
1/2 tsp pepper
1 shallot, finely chopped (about 1 Tbsp)
2 Tbsp freshly chopped basil
2 Tbsp lemon juice

MÂITRE D'HÔTEL BUTTER

1/4 cup butter, at room temperature
4 Tbsp chopped fresh parsley
1 shallot, finely chopped (about 1 Tbsp.)

SERVES 6-8

Combine ingredients for the marinade.

Place swordfish steaks in a shallow baking dish.

Pour marinade over steaks and allow to sit at room temperature for about 2 hours. Turn steaks over once during this time.

MAKE *MÂITRE D' HÔTEL* BUTTER
Blend all the ingredients well.

Form into a log about 2 inches diameter and roll up inches wax paper to cover. Chill in freezer.

Remove swordfish from marinade and shake off excess oil. Place steaks on grill.

Cook for 4 minutes on first side. Carefully flip steaks over and cook for 3 minutes more or until done.

Remove from grill, cut steaks in half, and put on warm plates.

Slice a pat of the maître d'hôtel butter for each steak and place it in the center of steak.

Serve with a slice of lemon.

BROILED FILLET OF TAUTOG (Blackfish) with Sauce Provençale

SERVES 4

Preheat broiler.

Prepare *sauce provençale* and set aside.

Place fillets on broiling rack (skin side up) and brush with clarified butter and sprinkle with bread crumbs.

Place under broiler and cook for about 4 minutes, skin side up. Turn fish once and continue to cook for 5 more minutes. Check fish for doneness.

Put the partially broiled tomatoes in the broiler and broil for another 2 minutes or so, making sure not to burn top of tomatoes. Serve at once when finished, with a suggested garnish of fresh sautéed string beans and a boiled potato.

Ingredients

4 fillets of tautog
sauce provençale
    (see p. 30)
2 medium size fresh
    tomatoes
1 oz bread crumbs
1 oz clarified fresh butter

BROILED FILLET OF TILEFISH with Grapefruit Beurre Blanc

Ingredients

4 fillets of tilefish
bread crumbs
salt and pepper to taste
2 oz oil or clarified butter
1 grapefruit, skinned, rind
    trimmed and separated
    into segments
beurre blanc (see p. 7)
1 Tbsp chives
1 Tbsp parsley

SERVES 4

Preheat broiler.

Make *beurre blanc*. To add grapefruit flavor, peel grapefruit with a fruit peeler or sharp knife.

Add the inside of the fruit without the rind and half of the segments before cooking. Strain the liquid.

Place fish fillets on a broiling rack, brushed with oil or clarified butter and broil skin side up for about 4 minutes

Turn fish once and continue to broil for another 4 minutes. Check fish for doneness. Fish should be opaque but still firm to the touch.

If fish is still not done, turn from broiler to oven setting, and continue to cook at 400 F for another 4 minutes.

When fish is cooked, ladle some of the *beurre blanc* onto a serving plate, place a tilefish fillet on it, and ladle a few tablespoons more of the *beurre blanc* sauce on top of fillet.

Place 3 segments of grapefruit on top.

TROUT
with Sour Cream Sauce

SERVES 4

Wash trout and pat them inside and out with a paper towel. Sprinkle insides with a little salt.

Dip trout in flour mixed with pepper and paprika.

Heat 2 Tbsp of the butter and the corn oil in a large heavy skillet until just sizzling.

Add trout and lower heat to medium.

Fry trout for about 4 or 5 minutes on each side until nicely browned, turning carefully with tongs.

Remove trout from skillet with a slotted spoon and keep warm on a heated platter.

Pour off all fat from the skillet and add the remaining 2 Tbsp butter.

Scrape up brown pan drippings with a spatula and heat to just sizzling.

Reduce heat and slowly stir in sour cream and lemon juice.

Cook over low heat for about 2 or 3 minutes, stirring constantly.

Ingredients

4 dressed trout (about 1/2–3/4 lb each)
salt
1/2 cup flour
dash of ground white pepper
pinch of paprika
4 Tbsp sweet butter (1/2 stick), divided
2 Tbsp corn oil
1 cup sour cream
1/2 tsp lemon juice
1 Tbsp fresh parsley, minced

GRILLED GOLDEN RAINBOW TROUT
with Lemon and Capers

Ingredients

4 14–16 oz whole
   boneless rainbow trout
2 oz canola oil
4 oz bread crumbs
3 lemons
3 oz capers
2 oz fresh butter

SERVES 4

Rub canola oil on fish and season with bread crumbs.

Grill for 2 minutes on each side.

Section three lemons and sauté in butter for 1 minute along with capers.

Place trout skin side up and place lemon and capers on top.

BLACKENED CATFISH
with Bourbon Pecan Butter

SERVES 4

MAKE BOURBON-PECAN BUTTER

In food processor or blender, grind pecans using pulse mode. The pecans should be fine, but leave in a few chunks.

Add room temperature butter .Add Bourbon, shallots, garlic, and red pepper. Mix all together.

Using a spatula, spoon out onto waxed paper and roll into a log. Refrigerate. Reserve for future use.

Mix all ingredients to make blackening spices. Preheat skillet (preferably a cast iron pan). Dredge fish fillets in spices, dip into oil and carefully set them on hot skillet.

Cook on first side for about 4 minutes, turn once, continue to cook for another 3–4 minutes. Place fish on warm serving platter or dishes.

Arrange fillets and top them with one or two slices of the Bourbon pecan butter (remove wax paper after cutting). Serve immediately with potatoes, rice, or any starch you may choose. A suggested vegetable is collard greens.

Ingredients

4 catfish fillets (about 8–10 oz each)

FOR BOURBON-PECAN BUTTER

1 Tbsp garlic, chopped
1/2 cup butte,r at room temperature
1/4 cup pecans finely ground
1/4 cup Bourbon
1 shallot, minced
1 Tbsp red pepper, diced

FOR BLACKENING SPICES

1 Tbsp paprika
2 1/2 tsp salt
1 tsp onion powder
1 tsp cayenne pepper
3/4 tsp white pepper
3/4 tsp ground black pepper
1/2 tsp dry thyme
1/2 tsp dry oregano

BROILED FILLET OF
SEA TROUT
with Fresh Lemon Thyme

Ingredients

4 whole sea trout, cleaned
and gutted
2 oz fresh lemon thyme
bread crumbs
2 oz clarified sweet butter

SERVES 4

Preheat broiler.

Chop lemon thyme very fine, leaving about 4 sprigs for garnish.

Mix chopped thyme in with the bread crumbs.

Pat sea trout dry, dip in bread crumbs and lemon thyme mixture.

Shake off excess.

Brush fish with clarified butter.

Place fish on broiling rack, skin side up, and broil 6 inches from the heat for about 4 to 5 minutes, until skin is crispy.

Turn once and brush again with clarified butter and continue to broil for another 5 minutes. Check for doneness.

Place fish on a warm serving plate, garnish with remaining fresh lemon thyme sprigs.

Serve hot at once with steamed potatoes.

TUNA STEAKS
with Olive Sauce

SERVES 4

Rub steaks on both sides with a well-blended mixture of salt, pepper, paprika, nutmeg, and dark brown sugar.

Melt butter in a large heavy skillet until just sizzling but not brown.

Pan broil tuna for about 5 minutes on each side or until the fish flakes easily with a fork.

Remove steaks to prewarmed plates with a slotted spoon.

Add olives and parsley to the butter in the skillet, and sauté for about 2 minutes.

Pour olive-butter mixture over the tuna steaks before serving.

Ingredients

4 fresh tuna steaks (1 inch thick and about 2–2 1/2 lb)
1 tsp salt
generous sprinkling of ground black pepper
1/2 tsp paprika
pinch of nutmeg
pinch of dark brown sugar
8 Tbsp (1 stick) sweet butter
1/4 cup pimiento-stuffed green olives, coarsely chopped
1/4 cup pitted black olives, coarsely chopped
1 Tbsp fresh parsley, minced

PENNE
with Sliced Tuna Steak and Fresh Tomatoes

Ingredients

1 lb penne
1 lb tuna steak, cut into 4
   portions
2 oz olive oil
1/2 Tbsp garlic, chopped
2 oz dry white wine
2 large tomatoes,
   chopped
1 Tbsp fresh basil,
   chopped
salt and pepper to taste

SERVES 4

Cook penne *al dente* and drain.

Grill tuna for 2–3 minutes each side or until medium rare.

Let sit 3 minutes and slice each piece into 4 slices.

In sauté pan place oil, garlic, white wine, tomatoes, and basil and reduce by one-third.

Add tuna and penne and heat for 1 minute.

Serve with salt and pepper.

BROILED ATLANTIC BLUEFIN TUNA STEAK
with Virgin Olive Oil and Fresh Chives

SERVES 4

Preheat broiler and broiling rack as well.

Brush fish with olive oil.

Place on hot rack and under the broiler for about 3 to 4 minutes on each side.

Place fish on warm serving plates and spoon some virgin olive oil on top.

Sprinkle with fresh chopped chives.

Cut steaks in half.

Serve immediately with salt and pepper to taste.

NOTE
Keep olive oil in warm place.

Ingredients

4 bluefin (or yellow fin) tuna steaks (10 oz each)
2 oz virgin olive oil
2 oz fresh chives, finely chopped
salt and pepper

BROILED ATLANTIC BLUEFIN TUNA STEAK
with Fresh Coriander Salsa

Ingredients

4 bluefin (or yellowfin)
   tuna fillets (10 oz each)
2 large tomatoes, seeded
   and diced
1 red onion, peeled and
   finely chopped
1 fresh jalapeño pepper,
   seeded and finely
   chopped
1 oz fresh coriander,
   chopped
2 oz virgin olive oil
1 oz lime juice
salt and pepper to taste

SERVES 4

PROCEDURE

Preheat broiler and broiling rack as well.

Brush fish with virgin olive oil.

Place tuna onto hot rack and under the broiler for about 3 or 4 minutes on each side.

TO MAKE SALSA

In a bowl, mix tomato, red onion, jalapeño, and fresh coriander.

Add olive oil, lime juice and salt and pepper.

Serve on the side with the fish.

SEARED NORTH ATLANTIC YELLOWFIN TUNA
with Garden Salad and Balsamic Vinaigrette

SERVES 4

black iron skillet.

Rub fresh lemon thyme on both sides of tuna steaks.

Sear with small amount of oil on both sides until desired doneness (about 3 minutes per side).

Make vinaigrette.

Slice each portion of tuna and place on plate with mesclun salad and radishes and drizzle vinaigrette over salad and tuna.

Serve at room temperature.

Ingredients

4 10 oz tuna steaks
1 oz fresh lemon thyme, chopped
basic vinaigrette (see p. 44)
1 lb mesclun salad
4 small red radishes

BROILED TURBOT FILLET
with Sea Urchin
Beurre Blanc

Ingredients

2 4 lb, whole turbot,
    skinned and filleted
2 oz canola oil
4 oz bread crumbs
4 oz uni (sea urchin roe)
salt and white pepper
beurre blanc (see p. 7)

SERVES 4

Lightly coat turbot fillets with bread crumbs and moisten with oil.

Broil each side for 2-3 minutes.

Make *beurre blanc.*

Add 3 oz sea urchin roe; salt and pepper to taste.

Strain and serve over fish with the remaining urchin roe as a garnish.

NORTH ATLANTIC TURBOT
Spinach and Salmon Ensemble

SERVES 4

Lightly pound slices of turbot and salmon. Broil each side for 2–3 minutes.

In a skillet, quickly sauté spinach leaves in 2 Tbsp butter with 4 oz of finely chopped shallots. Toss constantly. Spinach should remain firm, retaining its shape and color.

Make a bundle of first one slice of turbot, then salmon, then spinach, then salmon, and then finish with turbot.

Proceed to make the *beurre blanc*. Keep in a warm place.

In a mixing bowl, beat 4 whole eggs.

Dip bundle in flour, shake off excess, then cover with beaten eggs. Sauté fish in butter on a moderate to high flame for approximately 3 to 4 minutes per side.

When ready to serve, spoon a thin layer of *beurre blanc* sauce on a serving plate.

Garnish with chopped chives and diced tomato.

Ingredients

24 oz of turbot cut into 4 6 oz slices (2 per serving)
12 oz of salmon cut into 4 3 oz slices (2 per serving)
12 oz fresh spinach leaves
2 Tbsp butter
4 oz fresh shallots, finely chopped
4 eggs, beaten
2 Tbsp chopped chives
2 medium tomatoes, diced
beurre blanc (see p. 7)

POACHED IMPORTED NORTH SEA TURBOT FILLET
with Julienne of Fresh Vegetables

Ingredients

2 4 lb whole turbot,
  skinned and filleted
8 snow peas, julienned
1 celery stalk, julienned
1 leek, julienned
fish stock (see p. 48)

SERVES 4

Bring fish stock to the boil. Reduce heat.

Poach turbot fillets in fish stock for 3–4 minutes (do not bring to the boil).

Steam the julienned vegetables

Serve with hot vegetables and 2 Tbsp of the fish stock on top of fillets.

BROILED WHITEFISH
with Fresh
Lemon Thyme

SERVES 4

Preheat broiler.

Separate fresh lemon thyme leaves from the stem by rolling stems between the palms of your hands. Discard stems.

Mix thyme leaves with the bread crumbs.

Add salt and pepper to taste.

Dredge fillets in the fresh lemon thyme and bread crumb mixture.

Oil broiling rack. Place fillets on rack and broil for approximately 3 to 4 minutes.

Salt and pepper to taste.

NOTE
Whitefish cooks extremely fast. It also overcooks very quickly. Keep an eye on it.

Ingredients

4 skinless whitefish fillets
(about 8 oz each)
2 oz fresh lemon thyme
1 oz bread crumbs
salt and pepper

POACHED WHITING
with Anchovy Sauce

Ingredients

4 whiting fillets (about 2
   lb)
2 cups boiling water
1/4 tsp salt
dash of ground white
   pepper
4 Tbsp (1/4 stick) sweet
   butter
4 anchovy fillets, finely
   chopped
1/2 cup dry white wine
1 tsp fresh mint, minced
   (or dried mint may be
   used)
1 Tbsp fresh parsley,
   minced
1 Tbsp fresh lemon juice

SERVES 4

Pour boiling water into a large heavy skillet and place over low heat.

Season fillets with salt and pepper and gently add to the water.

Simmer for about 8 or 10 minutes until the fish flakes easily with a fork, but be careful not to overcook.

Meanwhile, melt butter in a small heavy saucepan and add anchovy fillets.

Sauté over low heat for about 5 minutes.

Stir in wine, mint, and parsley, and simmer for 2 or 3 minutes more.

Gently lift fish with a slotted spoon to prewarmed plates.

Spoon the anchovy sauce over fillets and sprinkle with lemon juice before serving.

BROILED FILLET OF WOLFFISH (LOUP) with Apple and Calvados

SERVES 4

Make the *beurre blanc* but add to ingredients 1 apple and the 2 oz of Calvados. When *beurre blanc* is ready, set aside for future use.

Preheat broiler.

Peel and core remaining 2 apples and, with a sharp knife, cut apples into disks about 1/2 inch thick.

Sauté apples in 2 Tbsp sweet butter until golden brown. Do not overcook; give apples some color but keep crisp. Set aside in a warm place.

Brush fish with clarified butter or oil.

Sprinkle with bread crumbs and place on broiling rack about 4 inches under the flame.

Broil for about 4 to 5 minutes. Turn fish once and continue to broil for another 4 minutes. Check for doneness.

Place on serving dish.

Garnish with 3 apple rings per portion. Ladle some apple *beurre blanc* on top and garnish with fresh finely chopped chives.

Ingredients

4 wolffish fillets
2 oz clarified sweet butter
  or vegetable oil
bread crumbs (unflavored)
3 red apples
2 Tbsp sweet butter
beurre blanc (see p. 7)
2 oz Calvados
4 sprigs fresh chives

BUFFET & SALAD

CAESAR SALAD

Ingredients

2 small heads romaine
    lettuce
1 cup water
1 egg
3/4 cup olive oil
3 garlic clove, crushed
1 tsp salt
generous sprinkling of
    ground black pepper
3 Tbsp red wine vinegar
l Tbsp Dijon mustard
dash of Worcestershire
1 tsp fresh lemon juice
3/4 cup Parmesan cheese,
    grated
1 Tbsp fresh parsley,
    minced
1 cup crisp croutons
6–7 anchovy fillets,
    cut into small pieces
2 hard-cooked eggs
    (optional), quartered

SERVES 8

Wash and thoroughly dry the lettuce.

Break or tear into small pieces in a large salad bowl and set aside.

Bring 1 cup water to a boil in a small saucepan.

Remove from heat, drop in the egg, and let stand for no more than 30 seconds.

Remove the egg from the water.

Put egg, oil, garlic, salt, pepper, vinegar, mustard, parsley, Worcestershire sauce, and lemon juice in a tightly covered jar.

Shake thoroughly and well.

Pour mixture over the lettuce and toss lightly. Sprinkle cheese, parsley, and croutons over all. Toss lightly once again.

Top with anchovy fillets and serve immediately while croutons are still crisp.

The salad may be garnished with quartered eggs.

CHEF'S SPECIAL SEAFOOD SALAD

SERVES 8

Wash and thoroughly dry the lettuce.

Separate and arrange the leaves on a chilled serving platter or on individual plates.

Make eight "cups" out of the inside leaves.

Place seafood attractively on the lettuce with tomatoes, olives, and eggs.

Fill the lettuce cups with cocktail sauce and place in the center of the serving plate.

Garnish with sprigs of parsley and lemon wedges.

NOTE
Any mayonnaise dressing or favorite seafood sauce may be substituted for the cocktail sauce.

Ingredients

2 heads bibb or Boston lettuce
1/2 lb blackfin crabmeat, cooked and chilled
1/2 lb lobster meat, cooked and chilled
16 jumbo shrimp, cooked, shelled, deveined, and chilled
l/2 lb halibut, cooked, flaked, and chilled
4 medium tomatoes, peeled and thinly sliced
8 large pitted black olives, thinly sliced
4large pitted green olives, thinly sliced
2 hard-cooked eggs, quartered
1–1 1/2 cups cocktail sauce (see p. 9)
8 sprigs of fresh parsley
2 lemons, cut in small wedges

COLESLAW

Ingredients

1/2 cup mayonnaise
    (see p. 23)
1 tsp salt
 ground white pepper to
    taste
2 Tbsp white vinegar
2 Tbsp sugar
1/2 tsp Dijon mustard
1 small head cabbage,
    finely shredded
1/4 cup shredded carrot
1 large green pepper,
    diced
1 large red pepper, diced
paprika

SERVES 4-6

Mix all ingredients together in a bowl.

Toss lightly and chill, tightly covered, for about 1 hour.

Sprinkle lightly with paprika before serving.

COLD POACHED DUNGENESS CRAB
with Mustard Mayonnaise

SERVES 4

Cook crabs in simmering *court bouillon* for 12-15 minutes.

Chill.

Remove tops of crabs and clean insides, replacing the tops once cleaned.

Make mustard mayonnaise by mixing mustard, mayonnaise, lemon juice, Worchestershire and seasonings.

Serve crabs with 2 oz mustard mayonnaise on side.

Ingredients

4 1-1/2 lb whole
    Dungeness crab, live
1 gallon *court bouillon*
    (see p. 11)
1 cup mayonnaise
    (see p. 23)
1/4 cup Dijon mustard
1 Tbsp Worchestershire
    sauce
1 dashes Tobasco
1 tsp lemon juice
salt and white pepper to
    taste

JUMBO LUMP CRAB SALAD
with Endives

Ingredients

20 oz imperial jumbo
    lump crabmeat
16 white endive leaves
16 red endive leaves
16 baby red oak leaves
16 baby lola rosa leaves
4 stalks celery, julienned
1 cup mayonnaise
    (see p. 23)
1/4 ketchup
1/4 cup Cognac
salt and pepper to taste
6 oz chives, half diced
    and half sticks

SERVES 4

Decorate each plate with 4 red endives, 4 white endives, 4 lola rosa leaves and 4 red oak leaves.

Make Cognac mayonnaise by mixing mayonnaise, Cognac, ketchup and salt and pepper.

Put a small bed of celery in center of plate and place 5 oz crabmeat and 2 oz Cognac mayonnaise on top of crab.

Garnish with chopped chives and chive sticks.

CRAB SALAD

SERVES 4

Combine all ingredients except mayonnaise, cream, lettuce, and pimiento strips in a large bowl.

Whisk mayonnaise and whipped cream together thoroughly.

Fold into the crabmeat and mix well.

Turn onto lettuce leaves.

Garnish with pimiento strips before serving.

Ingredients

1 lb backfin crabmeat,
    cooked and chilled
1 large stalk celery, diced
1 pimiento, minced
1 small onion, minced
2 hard-cooked eggs,
    finely chopped
salt to taste
ground white pepper to
    taste
1/2 cup mayonnaise
    (see p. 23)
1/2 cup heavy cream,
    whipped
4 lettuce leaves
1 pimiento, cut in thin
    strips

STONE CRABS
with Mustard Mayonnaise

SERVES 6

Make mustard mayonaise by mixing mustard mayonnaise, lemon juice, Worchestershire sauce, Tabasco sauce, and salt and pepper.

Lightly crack stone crab claw.

Serve stonecrab claws chilled with 2 oz mustard mayonnaise sauce and 2 oz clarified butter.

Ingredients

20 large stonecrab claws
1 cup mayonnaise
   (see p. 23)
1/2 cup Dijon mustard
1 Tbsp fresh lemon juice
1/2 tsp Worcestershire
   sauce
5 drops Tabasco sauce
salt and pepper to taste
8 oz sweet clarified butter

DUTCH HERRING
and Beet Salad

Ingredients

3 Matjes herring, boned, skinned (optional), and diced
cold water or milk
1 medium-large onion, coarsely chopped
4 medium beets, cooked, peeled, and diced
2 apples, peeled, cored, and diced
1 small dill pickle, minced
1 large stalk celery, thinly sliced
1/2 cup corn oil
1/4 cup wine vinegar
1 tsp Dijon mustard
1 Tbsp sugar
1 garlic clove, crushed or minced
ground black pepper to taste
6 large lettuce leaves
chopped walnuts

SERVES 6

Freshen the whole herring, boned and skinned (optional), in cold water or milk for 24 hours.

Be sure the fish is completely covered with water/milk and change the liquid 3 or 4 times during the freshening.

Remove the herring and pat dry with a paper towel.

Cut into bite-size pieces.

Combine the herring in a large bowl with all other ingredients except lettuce leaves and quartered eggs.

Toss lightly but well.

Cover the bowl tightly and chill thoroughly in the refrigerator for at least 5 hours.

Toss lightly onto lettuce leaves before serving. Garnish with chopped walnuts.

SALAD OF RAY
with Radicchio, Frisée, Mache & Tarragon Dressing

SERVES 8

Poach ray in *court bouillon* for 10–12 minutes.

Remove and cut 1 inch-thick strips along the seams.
Mix together mache, frisée and radicchio.

Make tarragon dressing.

Add greens and the tarragon dressing.

In alternating layers, place greens in center of plate
and top with ray and red pepper.

Pour 1 oz of dressing on top and garnish with capers.

Ingredients

4 large ray (skate) wings,
    filleted and skinned
1 head radicchio, cleaned
    and cut into 1in-cubes
2 heads Italian frisée,
    cleaned and cut into
    1 inch cubes
8 heads mache, cleaned
tarragon dressing
    (see p. 38)
1 red pepper, cut into 1/4
    inch strips lengthwise
4 Tbsp capers
4 cups *court bouillon*
    (see p. 11)

SALMON SALAD

Ingredients

1 lb salmon, cooked and
    flaked, or canned
    salmon may be used
    instead
1 stalk celery, thinly sliced
1 small onion, minced
1/2 cup red cabbage, finely
    chopped
1/2 cup sweet pickles,
    drained and minced
1 1/2 tsp salt
dash ground black pepper
1 Tbsp horseradish
1 small head romaine lettuce
1 Tbsp sugar
2 tsp dry mustard
pinch of cayenne
3/4 cup corn oil
1 egg
1/4 cup wine vinegar
3 Tbsp cornstarch
1 cup cold water
4 radishes, thinly sliced
2 hard-cooked eggs, thinly
    sliced
1 Tbsp fresh parsley, minced

SERVES 4

Lightly toss salmon, celery, onion, cabbage, pickles, 3/4 tsp salt, pepper, and horseradish in a large bowl.

Line a large salad bowl with romaine leaves. Turn the salmon salad onto the leaves.

Cover tightly and refrigerate while you make the dressing.

Make dressing. Put sugar, mustard, 3/4 tsp salt, cayenne, oil, egg, and vinegar in a large bowl. Set aside.

Blend cornstarch and water in a small saucepan, and thoroughly mix.

Cook the cornstarch and water over low heat until the mixture boils and becomes clear, stirring constantly. Remove from heat and briskly whisk into the ingredients in the bowl.

When the dressing is smooth, drizzle it over the salmon salad. Toss lightly in the salad bowl and garnish with radishes.

Arrange eggs around the salad bowl.

Sprinkle parsley over all.

SALAD NIÇOISE

SERVES 4-6

Boil the red potatoes 20 minutes or until done

Peel the red onions and cut into thin rings.

Put salad in bowl.

Add thke radishes and Niçoise olives.
Peel, wash and dry the radishes and black olives Add
the grilled peppers.

Prepare sauce vinaigrette (see p. 45).

Rub a wooden salad bowl with a clove of peeled
garlic, put sauce vinaigrette at the bottom, then mx in
all the ingredients, including the tuna and anchovies.

Garnish with chopped parsley.

Mix at the last moment and. Place on plate in large
mound. Garnish with more olives, capers and anchovy
fillets on top

Ingredients
3 small red potatoes,
    peeled and quartered
4 cups mesclun salad
6 oz canned tuna in oil
2 sweet peppers (mix
    colors)
1 large red onion
6 medium tomatoes
6 artichoke hearts,
    quartered

5 red radishes
2 oz black olives
4 oz *sauce vinaigrette*
    (see p. 45)
1 garlic clove
6 anchovy filets in oil
3 sprigs parsely
basil
salt and pepper to taste

MARINATED SHRIMP & CALAMARI SALAD VINAIGRETTE

Ingredients

16 medium shrimp,
   cleaned and deveined
1/2 calamari (bodies
   only), cleaned
salt and pepper to taste
1 to 2 Tbsp olive oil
1 head of red leaf lettuce,
   cleaned and dry
24 thin strips of sweet red
   pimienos
1 3/4 cups sauce
   vinaigrette (see p. 45)

SERVES 4-6

Season shrimp with salt and pepper to taste.

Heat olive oil in a heavy sauté pan over moderate heat.

When oil is hot, add shrimp and sauté for 2 or 3 minutes or until pink. Remove from pan and set aside to cool.

Blanch calimari in a pot of boiling, salted water for 20 to 30 seconds or until they begin to turn opaque. Remove from water with a slotted spoon and rinse under cold water. Slice into rings. Set aside to cool.

Combine calimari and shrimps with vinaigrette. Refrigerate for a least 1 hour. Arrange some lettuce leaves on each plate. Add some marinated seafood to each plate (6 shrimps per serving). Drizzle several teaspoons of the marinating liquid around edges of the plate. Garnish with strips of red, sweet pimientos.

SCALLOP SALAD

SERVES 4

Bring water, wine, *bouquet garni*, salt, pepper, and onion to a boil in a large, heavy saucepan.

Add scallops and reduce heat.

Simmer for 2-3 minutes until scallops are opaque.

Strain scallops and pat dry with a paper towel.

Discard liquid and *bouquet garni*.

Set scallops aside in a bowl and let cool.

When cool add mayonnaise, celery, and pickles.

Toss lightly and refrigerate for 1 hour tightly covered.

Turn onto lettuce leaves and garnish with sprigs of parsley before serving.

Ingredients)

2 cups water
1 cup dry white wine
bouquet garni: 1 bay leaf, 1/2 tsp thyme, 1 Tbsp fresh parsley, coarsely chopped. Wrap tightly in a piece of cheesecloth.
1/2 tsp salt
dash of ground white pepper
1 small onion, coarsely chopped
1 lb bay scallops
1 cup mayonnaise (see p. 23)
1 stalk celery, minced
1/4 cups sweet pickles, drained and minced
4 lettuce leaves
4 sprigs of fresh parsley

SCALLOPS SEVICHE

Ingredients

2 qt boiling water
2 lb bay scallops
1 cup fresh lemon juice
1/2 cup fresh orange
    juice
1/2 cup fresh lime juice
1 large onion, thinly sliced
1 large hot red pepper, cut
    in thin strips (or 1 Tbsp
    dried red pepper
    flakes)
4 lettuce leaves
1 Tbsp fresh parsley,
    minced

SERVES 8

Pour boiling water over scallops in a colander. Drain well and pat dry with a paper towel.

Place scallops in a large bowl and cover completely with the fruit juices.

Add onion and pepper and toss lightly to distribute the flavors. Cover tightly and refrigerate for 5 or 6 hours.

Strain scallops and discard juice and vegetables.

Arrange scallops on the lettuce leaves.

Sprinkle with parsley before serving.

SHRIMP SALAD

SERVES 6

Sauté shrimp and garlic in 1/4 cup of the olive oil in a large, heavy skillet for about 5 minutes.

Turn the shrimp carefully with tongs while sautéing.

Discard the garlic and pour off the oil into a large bowl.

Add the remaining 3/4 cup oil, lemon juice, salt, pepper, cayenne, and red pepper flakes.

Mix well and add shrimp.

Cover tightly and refrigerate for 1 hour.

Toss shrimp and dressing lightly but well and turn onto Romaine leaves.

Garnish with slices of onion and orange. Sprinkle with parsley before serving.

Ingredients

1–1 1/2 lb jumbo shrimp, cooked, shelled, deveined, and split
1 garlic clove, coarsely chopped
1 cup olive oil
1/4 cup fresh lemon juice
1 tsp salt
sprinkling of ground white pepper
pinch of cayenne
1/2 tsp dried red pepper flakes
1 small head Romaine lettuce
1 medium Bermuda onion, thinly sliced
1 medium-large orange, thinly sliced
1 Tbsp fresh parsley, minced

SHRIMP AND
SCALLOP SALAD
with Mushrooms

Ingredients

1/2 cup olive oil
1/2 cup fresh lemon juice
1/2 tsp salt
generous sprinkling of
    ground black pepper
pinch of cayenne
1 Tbsp honey
1/2 lb mushrooms, thinly
    sliced
1 lb shrimp, cooked,
    shelled, and deveined
1 lb raw bay scallops,
    chilled
1 lb fresh spinach, washed
    and picked over with
    stems removed
1 Tbsp fresh parsley,
    minced

SERVES 8

Thoroughly whisk oil, lemon juice, salt, pepper, cayenne, and honey together in a large bowl.

Add the mushrooms and toss lightly but coat well.

Arrange shrimp and scallops on a bed of raw spinach leaves.

Top with the mushrooms and dressing.

Sprinkle with parsley before serving.

TUNA SALAD

Ingredients

1/2 cup mayonnaise
  (see p. 23)
1/2 tsp salt
sprinkling of ground white
  pepper
1 Tbsp white vinegar
2 scallions with tops, thinly
  sliced
1 small stalk celery, thinly
  sliced
1 small cucumber, peeled,
  seeded, and diced
1 pimiento, finely chopped
1 hard-cooked egg, finely
  chopped
1 lb tuna, cooked and
  flaked, or canned tuna
  may be used instead
4 lettuce leaves
paprika
2 tomatoes, peeled and
  quartered
8 pimiento-stuffed olives

SERVES 4

Combine mayonnaise, salt, pepper, and vinegar in a large bowl.

Add scallions, celery, cucumber, pimiento, egg, and tuna.

Toss lightly but well.

Refrigerate, tightly covered, for 1 hour.

Turn onto lettuce leaves and sprinkle with paprika.

Garnish with tomatoes and olives.

LOBSTER SALAD

SERVES 4

In a large pot, steam all the 1lb lobsters 7 minutes.
Chill. A 11/2 lb lobster requires proportionately more
time. When cool enough to handle, clean each lobster.
Remove the meat from the tails, break the claws open
and remove each piece of meat intact. Save the legs
from each. Keep the meat from each lobster separate
so that when plating the salad, each serving will consist
of a whole lobster.

TO MAKE THE DRESSING

In a metal bowl, combine the egg yolks, shallots, curry
powder, salt, pepper, and vinegar.

Slowly whisk in the oil until ingredients are combined
and the dressing thickens.

Mix in the chopped fresh tarragon. Wash the salad
greens and spin them dry.

Chop and mix them together. Toss with some of the
dressing. When ready to serve, put a bed of the
lettuces in the middle of each plate.

Arrange the claw meat and the legs around the salad
to look like a lobster. Slice the tail meat and place it on
top of mixed greens.

Ingredients

4 1lb lobsters
2 heads of frisée
4 bunches mache
2 heads of radicchio

FOR THE DRESSING

3 egg yolks
1 medium shallot, finely
   chopped
1 tsp curry powder
1/3 cup tarragon vinegar
salt and pepper to taste
1 cup vegetable oil
2 oz fresh tarragon, finely
   chopped

LOBSTER PARFAIT

Ingredients

1/2 cup basic mayonnaise
(see p. 23)
3 Tbsp chili sauce
1 tsp fresh lemon juice
1 Tbsp fresh chives,
minced
1/2 tsp horseradish
1 Tbsp celery, minced
1 lb lobster meat, cooked
and chilled
1 small head lettuce,
leaves and shredded

SERVES 4

Thoroughly mix mayonnaise, chili sauce, lemon juice, chives, horseradish, and celery in a large bowl.

Add lobster meat and refrigerate tightly covered for about 30 minutes.

Into the bottom of 4 tall, chilled parfait glasses sprinkle shredded lettuce leaves, and line the sides with unshredded lettuce leaves.

Toss lobster lightly but well and spoon into the glasses to serve.

NOTE
Cocktail sauce (see p. 9) may be used instead of the mayonnaise dressing.

SALMON MOUSSE
with Sauce Vert
(Green Sauce)

SERVES 6-8

Soften the gelatin in cold water.

Add boiling water and stir until the gelatin is dissolved.

Set gelatin aside and let cool.

When the gelatin is cool add mayonnaise, lemon juice, onion, Tabasco sauce, paprika, and salt.

Mix thoroughly and chill until just beginning to thicken. Add salmon and capers and combine thoroughly.

Fold in whipped cream and pour salmon mixture into a lightly oiled fish or other decorative mold.

Chill until set.

Unmold the mousse on a serving platter.

Garnish with watercress and serve *sauce vert* on the side.

Ingredients

1 envelope unflavored
    gelatin
1/4 cup cold water
1/2 cup boiling water
1/2 cup mayonnaise
    (see p. 23)
1 Tbsp fresh lemon juice
1 Tbsp onion, grated
1/2 tsp Tabasco sauce
1/2 tsp paprika
1 tsp salt
1 lb salmon, cooked,
    drained, and finely
    chopped
1 Tbsp capers, finely
    chopped
1/2 cup heavy cream,
    whipped
bunch of watercress
1–1 1/2 cups *sauce vert*
    or green sauce
    (see p.16)

COLD SHRIMP CURRY
with White Grapes

Ingredients

1 or 2 Tbsp curry powder
    to taste
1 cup mayonnaise (see p.
    23)
dash of cayenne
sprinkling of ground white
    pepper
3/4 cup seedless white
    grapes
1 1/4 lb shrimp, cooked,
    shelled, deveined, and
    chilled
bunch of watercress
1/2 cup blanched
    almonds, slivered
chutney

SERVES 4-6

Thoroughly mix curry powder, mayonnaise, cayenne, and pepper in a bowl.

Add white grapes and toss lightly but well.

Pour mayonnaise and grapes over shrimp.

Refrigerate shrimp, tightly covered, for 1 hour.

Toss lightly onto a bed of watercress.

Sprinkle slivered almonds on top before serving.

Serve side dishes of a favorite chutney with the curry.

MARINATED SEA SCALLOPS AND MUSSELS
in a Mustard Vinaigrette on Fresh Avocado

SERVES 6-8

Prepare the mustard vinaigrette.

In a bowl, combine the chilled mussels and drained scallops with about 1/2 of the prepared vinaigrette.

Cover and refrigerate.

Prepare the marinade in a mixing bowl by combining the white wine water, and lime or lemon. Put the scallops and mussels into the martinade and let it marinate for about 24 hours for the best flavor.

When ready to serve, cut each avocado in half. Peel and remove the pit.

Brush with a little olive oil or lemon juice to retard discoloration. For each serving, place half an avocado on a bed of multi-colored lettuce leaves.

Spoon seafood mixture into the halves, allowing it to spill over the sides.

Spoon remaining vinaigrette over each serving to taste.

Sprinkle with fresh chopped parsley and serve.

Ingredients

- 1 lb mussels, scrubbed and bearded
- 1 lb sea scallops cut into bite-sized pieces (or1 lb bay scallops, whole)
- 1/2 cup white wine
- 1/2 cup water
- 1/2 cup fresh lime or lemon juice
- 3 medium avocados
- 2 Tbsp olive oil or lemon juice
- a variety of various colored lettuces to create beds for the avocado halves
- 1 tsp fresh parsley, finely chopped
- 1 1/2 cups mustard vinaigrette (see p. 45)

COD FILLETS
with Horseradish Sauce

Ingredients

1/4 cup horseradish
   sauce (p. 10)
4 cod fillets (about 2 lb),
   cooked and chilled
4 lettuce leaves
2 hard-cooked eggs,
   quartered
2 tomatoes, peeled and
   thinly sliced
1 Tbsp dill, choppedl

SERVES 4

Prepare horseradish sauce.

Arrange chilled cod fillets in a shallow dish in a single layer.

Pour the horseradish sauce over the fish.

Cover tightly and marinate in the refrigerator for 1 hour.

Place each fish fillet carefully on a lettuce leaf and cover with the horseradish sauce.

Garnish with the quartered eggs and sliced tomatoes.

Sprinkle the tablespoon of dill which has not gone into the horseradish sauce over all.

SHRIMP RÉMOULADE

SERVES 6

Slice shrimp and sprinkle with lemon juice, paprika, salt, and pepper.

Cover tightly and refrigerate.

Put all remaining ingredients in the order given in a jar with a lid.

Mix the oil in a little at a time, stirring well after each addition.

Cover the jar tightly and shake it vigorously until the rémoulade is thoroughly blended.

Chill for 2 or 3 hours.

Arrange shrimp on lettuce leaves and pour rémoulade over all. Garnish with minced parsley before serving.

Ingredients

1 1/2 lb jumbo shrimp, cooked, shelled, deveined, chilled, and sliced
juice from 1 large lemon
1 tsp paprika
1 tsp salt
generous sprinkling of ground black pepper
1/2 cup tarragon vinegar
1 Tbsp chili sauce
1 or 2 scallions, thinly sliced
1 garlic clove, minced or mashed
1/4 cup celery, finely chopped
1 tsp dry mustard
1 1/4 cups olive oil
1 small head lettuce
1 Tbsp fresh parsley, minced

SIDE DISHES

OVEN FRENCH FRIES

Ingredients

3–4 large potatoes, peeled
    and cut into 1/2inch
    strips
1 qt ice water
1/4 cup corn oil
salt to taste
ground white pepper to
    taste

SERVES 6-8

Preheat oven to 450 F.

Soak potato strips in ice water for 15 minutes.

Pour off water and thoroughly dry potatoes on paper towels.

Spread the potato strips in a single layer on a baking sheet or in a shallow baking dish.

Pour oil over them and toss lightly to coat well.

Bake for about 35 minutes until nicely browned.

Turn the potato strips carefully several times to be sure they bake evenly.

Drain on a paper towel and season with salt and pepper.

HUSH PUPPIES

SERVES 6-8

Heat oil for deep frying to 375 F in a large, heavy kettle or skillet. A piece of bread dropped into the oil will turn golden brown when the temperature of the oil is just right.

Thoroughly mix cornmeal, flour, baking powder, and salt in a large bowl.

Whisk in and blend beaten egg, milk, half-and-half, and onion, until thickened.

Form the mixture into small cones or balls.

Fry in deep fat until golden brown and crispy.

Remove hush puppies with a slotted spoon and drain on paper towels before serving.

Ingredients

corn oil for deep frying
2 cups cornmeal
1 Tbsp flour
2 Tbsp baking powder
1 tsp salt
1 egg, beaten
1 cup milk
1 cup half-and-half
1 small onion, minced

FRENCH-FRIED ONION RINGS

Ingredients

4 large onions
1 cup milk
1 cup ice water
1 cup all-purpose flour (or
    dry pancake mix may
    be used instead, as a
    heavier batter)
corn oil for deep frying
salt
ground white pepper

SERVES 6-8

Peel and slice onions about 1/4 inch thick.

Separate the slices into rings.

Soak the onions in milk and ice water for 1 hour.

Pour off milk and water and pat the onions dry on a paper towel.

Dip the rings into flour/pancake mix, coating well.

Heat oil in a large, heavy skillet or Dutch oven to 375 F. A piece of bread dropped into the oil will turn golden when the temperature of the oil is just right.

Drop the onion rings a few at a time into the oil.

Fry until golden brown.

Drain on a paper towel and season with salt and pepper.

OYSTER BAR BISCUITS

SERVES 20

Preheat oven to 375 F.

Sift flour, baking powder, and salt together in a large bowl.

Cut in the shortening and mix until well blended.

Add milk and knead the dough until smooth and soft.

Form dough into 20 biscuits approximately 2 1/2 inches in diameter.

Place on a cookie sheet which has been covered with parchment and bake for about 15 minutes, or until golden brown.

Ingredients

6 cups flour
2 Tbsp baking powder
1 Tbsp salt
I/2 cup vegetable
    shortening
1 cup buttermilk

HASHED BROWN POTATOES

Ingredients

3–4 large potatoes,
peeled, cooked, cooled,
and coarsely chopped
(boiled or
baked–leftovers are
allowed)
3 Tbsp all-purpose flour
1/4 cup light cream
1 tsp salt
generous sprinkling of
ground black pepper
1 small onion, minced
3 Tbsp corn oil
1 Tbsp sweet butter

SERVES 6-8

Lightly mix potatoes in a bowl with flour and pour cream over them.

Season with salt and pepper and mix in onion.

Heat 2 Tbsp of the corn oil in a 9-inch heavy skillet over medium heat.

Add potatoes and press them down with a spatula into a flat cake.

Fry potatoes until crusty and nicely browned, shaking the skillet to keep them from sticking.

Lift potatoes carefully from the skillet with a spatula onto a preheated plate.

Wipe any crumbs from the skillet and add to it the remaining 1 Tbsp oil and the butter.

Slide potato cake back into the skillet, browned side up.

Fry until the underside is crusty and brown, shaking the skillet and pressing down the edges of the potato cake with a spatula.

BOILED NEW POTATOES
with Parsley Butter

SERVES 4

Drop potatoes into a heavy saucepan with enough boiling salted water to cover them.

Cover the saucepan and cook the potatoes until just tender, about 20 minutes.

Drain off water from the potatoes and peel them carefully.

NOTE
Leave the skins on if you prefer. Many people insist that the tender skins add to the enjoyment of eating new potatoes.

Heat butter and parsley in a skillet.

Add the potatoes and shake them to coat well with parsley butter.

Ingredients

12 small new potatoes with their skins
1/2 tsp salt
boiling water
6 Tbsp (3/4 stick) sweet butter
1 Tbsp fresh parsley, minced

BROILED OR BAKED TOMATO HALVES

Ingredients

4 large tomatoes
salt
ground black pepper
1 Tbsp fresh butter
1 tsp fresh tarragon,
    minced
1 tsp fresh chervil, minced
1 Tbsp fresh parsley,
    minced

SERVES 4

NOTE
Grated cheese or bread crumbs may be sprinkled on the tomato halves, or almost anything else that seems interesting, for both the tomatoes and the fish you are serving.

Preheat oven (if you're baking the tomatoes) to 425 F.

Cut out the cores from the stem end of the tomatoes, and slice them in half.

Place the tomatoes in a shallow baking dish or a baking sheet that can be put under the broiler.

Make cross-cuts on the top of each tomato and season with salt and pepper.

Divide butter into 8 small pats, and push 1 pat into each tomato half.

Sprinkle each half with tarragon, chervil, and parsley.

Place the tomatoes under the broiler for about 8 or 10 minutes, until they are tender and the tops are lightly browned or bake for about 15 minutes until the tomato halves are browned as above.

PAN-FRIED TOMATOES

SERVES 6-8

Slice tomatoes about 1/2 in thick.

Season with salt and pepper.

Dip the tomatoes in egg and then in bread crumbs, coating well.

Heat butter and oil in a large, heavy skillet until just sizzling.

Fry tomato slices quickly until nicely browned on both sides.

Turn carefully with a spatula.

Drain on a paper towel.

Ingredients

4 large tomatoes,
    green or red
salt
ground black pepper
2 eggs, beaten
1 cup fine bread crumbs
8 Tbsp (1 stick)
    sweet butter
1 Tbsp peanut oil

DESSERTS

APPLE ALMOND TART

Ingredients

FOR THE FILLING

6 Granny Smith apples,
    peeled cored and sliced
    thin
2 oz browned butter
2 oz granulated sugar
1 oz Calvados brandy

FOR THE TOPPING

2 1/4 cups granulated
    sugar
1 oz all-purpose flour
2 medium eggs
1 oz melted butter
1/4 tsp vanilla extract
3 1/2 sliced blanched
    almonds
powdered sugar

SERVES 6-8

TO MAKE THE FILLING
Half bake a 10-inch tart pan lined with puff pastry
rolled at 1/8 inch thick.

Brown the butter in a sauté pan and add apples and
sugar.

Cook until *al dente*.

Pour in the Calvados brandy and cook off excess.

Spread evenly into the half-baked shell.

TO MAKE THE TOPPING

Whisk sugar and flour together.

Add the melted butter and mix until absorbed.

Add eggs and vanilla extract and mix smooth.

Add the sliced almonds and pour over apples, spread
evenly and bake at 350 F until golden brown.

Dust with powdered sugar, cut and serve.

WHOLE WHEAT APPLE PIE

SERVES 10

PASTRY

Thoroughly mix flour and shortening in a large bowl. Combine all other ingredients with flour and shortening and mix well, kneading dough quickly and lightly into a smooth ball. Divide the ball in 2 pieces and refrigerate each wrapped in wax paper for 1 or 2 hours.

FILLING

Place apple slices in a large heavy saucepan and partly cover with water. Simmer for approximately 10 minutes.

Drain off water and refrigerate apple slices for 30 minutes. Combine sugar, flour, cinnamon, nutmeg, and lemon juice. Mix apple slices well with other ingredients.

Preheat oven to 350 F.

Roll out one ball of the dough flat and fit it gently into an 11-inch pie plate. Put the apples into the pie plate.

Roll out the second ball of dough flat and fit it over the apples, pressing the edges of the dough together around the rim.

Trim off any excess dough and cut a gash in the top crust. Brush top of pie with egg yolk and bake for approximately 1 hour or until golden brown.

Ingredients

PASTRY

3 1/2 cups whole wheat flour
1 cup all-purpose flour, sifted
1 1/2 cups vegetable shortening
1/4 cup water
2 eggs, beaten well
3/4 cup sugar
generous dash of salt
pin of baking soda

FILLING

5 lb apples, peeled, cored, and sliced
1 1/2 cups sugar
2 Tbsp flour
1 Tbsp cinnamon
1/2 Tbsp ground nutmeg
1 1/2 Tbsp fresh lemon juice
1 egg yolk

BANANA STRIP

Ingredients

BOTTOM
10 oz puff pastry (may be
   purchased from a
   bakery)

SERVES 6

Preheat oven to 350 F.

Roll out the puff pastry on cooking parchment to a strip
approximately 16 inches long, 6 inches wide, and 1/8
inch thick.

Chill the pastry for 30 minutes in the refrigerator.

Bake for 25 minutes or until the pastry is crisp.

Set aside to cool.

MAKE FILLING (see p. 329).

Cover the pastry strip with the cream filling and top
with sliced bananas.

Cook the apricot topping in a small heavy saucepan
over low heat, for about 10 minutes.

Brush the apricot topping over the bananas.

Decorate the strip with the remaining whipped cream.

MAKE FILLING (CON'T.)

Beat the egg with 1/4 cup of the milk and thoroughly mix in cornstarch.

Combine the remaining milk and sugar and bring to a boil in a small heavy saucepan.

Remove from heat and gradually pour the hot milk in a slow stream into the egg mixture while beating rapidly. Return all ingredients to the saucepan.

Cook over medium heat until the mixture is thick.

Whisk rapidly to avoid scorching the mixture.

Pour thickened cream filling into a bowl and brush melted butter on top.

Refrigerate until chilled.

Beat heavy cream until soft peaks form.

Beat the cream filling thoroughly, and carefully fold in half the whipped cream.

Ingredients (cont'd)

FILLING

1 egg
4 cups milk
5 Tbsp cornstarch
5 Tbsp sugar
2 Tbsp (1/4 stick) sweet
    butter, melted
2 cups heavy cream

TOPPING

2–3 bananas, sliced
5 oz (10 Tbsp) apricot
    topping

BLUEBERRY PIE

Ingredients

PASTRY

2 1/2 cups all-purpose
   flour, sifted
1 tsp baking powder
1/2 cup sugar
2 tsp pure vanilla extract
2 eggs, beaten well
1 cup (2 sticks) butter, cut
   in small pieces and
   softened

SERVES 6 OR MORE

PASTRY

Sift the flour and baking powder together on a wooden board. Make a well in the center of the flour.

Put sugar, vanilla, and eggs in the well.

Mix flour in from the sides to form a thick and creamy paste.

Put softened butter on top of the paste and cover with the remaining flour.

Knead dough quickly and lightly until all ingredients form a smooth ball.

Divide the ball in 2 pieces and refrigerate each wrapped in wax paper.

FILLING

Sprinkle blueberries with sugar, flour, lemon rind, and lemon juice, and let stand for 15 minutes in a bowl.

Preheat oven to 450 F.

Roll out one ball of the dough flat and fit it gently into a 10-inch pie plate (with a wide-channeled rim to catch juices).

Put the berries into the pie plate.

Roll out the second ball of dough flat and fit it over the berries, pressing the edges of the dough together around the rim.

Trim off any excess dough and cut a gash in the top crust.

Bake pie for 45–60 minutes until the crust is golden brown and the berries are tender.

Serve plain, or with vanilla ice cream or a dollop of whipped cream.

Ingredients (con't)

FILLING

4 cups fresh blueberries,
    washed and sorted
3/4–1 cup sugar
1/4 cup flour
1/2 tsp grated lemon rind
2 Tbsp fresh lemon juice

BUTTERSCOTCH SAUCE

Ingredients

1 egg yolk
4 Tbsp 1/2 stick) sweet
   butter
1/4 cup water
2/3 cup light brown sugar
1/3 cup corn syrup

MAKES ABOUT 1 CUP

Separate egg and set the white aside for another use.

In the top part of a double boiler, away from the heat, whisk the egg yolk briskly until thick and creamy.

Add butter, water, brown sugar, and corn syrup, and mix well.

Cook over boiling water, stirring constantly until mixture forms a thick syrup.

Remove from heat, and beat thoroughly until the sauce is creamy.

CHARLOTTE RUSSE
AU CHOCOLAT

SERVES 5 OR MORE

Soften gelatin in cold water for 5 minutes.

Melt chocolate over very low heat and add boiling water, stirring constantly until thickened and smooth.

Add sugar, salt, and milk, and continue cooking and stirring over low heat for 2 or 3 minutes.

Remove chocolate mixture from heat and stir in gelatin until it is dissolved.

Let chocolate mixture cool until it begins to thicken.

Whip the heavy cream until soft peaks form.

Fold the whipped cream into the chocolate mixture and stir in vanilla.

Line a round, oval, or other mold with ladyfingers.

Pour the chocolate mixture into the mold and chill until firm.

Unmold before serving.

Ingredients

2 tsp unflavored gelatin
2 Tbsp cold water
1 oz unsweetened
   chocolate
1/4 cup boiling water
1/4 cup plus 2 Tbsp sugar
pinch of salt
3/4 cup evaporated milk
1 cup heavy cream
1/2–1 tsp pure vanilla
   extract
10 ladyfingers

CHEESECAKE

Ingredients

THE PASTRY

1 cup sugar
7/8 cup butter
2 eggs, beaten
pinch salt
1/2–3/4 tsp lemon rind
1 3/4 cup all-purpose flour

SERVES 10

PASTRY

Combine sugar and butter in a large bowl and mix well.

Blend in eggs, salt, and lemon rind.

Add sift flour and thoroughly mix all ingredients into a ball.

Wrap the dough in wax paper or foil and refrigerate for 2 hours.

Roll out the chilled dough with a floured rolling pin in a circle approximately 18 inches in diameter and 1/8 inch thick.

Roll dough onto the floured rolling pin.

Place rolling pin over a lightly greased cake pan 10 inches in diameter and 2 1/2 inches deep.

Unroll the dough and gently press it around the sides of the cake pan.

Trim dough all around pan approximately 1/4 inch below the edge of the pan.

FILLING

Preheat oven to 325 F.

Combine cream cheese, vanilla, salt, lemon juice, and sugar in a large bowl.

Mix carefully with a rubber spatula, but do not beat.

Thoroughly blend 2 egg at a time into the cheese mixture, until it's firm.

Put the cheese filling into the pastry shell and bake for approximately 30 minutes, or until cake is golden brown

Ingredients (cont'd)

FILLING
3 lbs, 12 oz cream cheese (use only a very firm brand)
1–2 drops of pure vanilla extract
pinch salt
1 Tbsp fresh lemon juice
2 cups sugar
6 eggs

DUTCH ALMOND CAKE

Ingredients

FILLING

11 oz almond paste
12 Tbsp (1 1/2 sticks)
    sweet butter
3 eggs
1/4 cup flour
1 tsp lemon extract
commercial raspberry jam
1 cup sliced almonds
candied cherries

SERVES 10

PASTRY

Follow the recipe for Cheescake (p. 334).

FILLING

Preheat oven to 350 F.

Thoroughly blend almond paste with 4 Tbsp of the butter in a large bowl.

Beat in remaining butter, mixing well to be sure there are no lumps.

When smooth, blend in eggs one at a time, then flour and lemon extract.

Spread the bottom of the prepared dough with raspberry jam.

Carefully pour in the filling and sprinkle with sliced almonds.

Bake for approximately 1 hour or until golden brown. Decorate with candied cherries.

OLD-FASHIONED FRENCH VANILLA ICE CREAM

MAKES ABOUT 2 QUARTS

In the top part of a double boiler away from the heat, whisk egg yolks and milk until well blended.

Stir in sugar, salt, and the vanilla bean.

Cook, stirring constantly, over hot but not boiling water. When mixture is thick and creamy, remove from heat and cool. Cover and refrigerate until chilled.

NOTE
If vanilla extract is used, add after cooking. Stir in vanilla extract, or remove the vanilla bean and scrape the insides into the chilled custard mixture.

Pour the mixture into a container and place in freezer until partially frozen and mushy, about 1 hour.

Whip the heavy cream until soft peaks form.

Pour custard mixture into a chilled bowl 9 use the freezer container if it is large enough). Beat the mixture until smooth and creamy. Fold in the whipped cream and blend well.

Pour into 1 or 2 large freezer containers, leaving about 1 inch at the top. Cover and freeze until firm, about 3 hours.

Ingredients

6 egg yolks
2 cups milk
1 cup sugar
1/4 tsp salt
1 vanilla bean, split lengthwise (or 2 Tbsp pure vanilla extract may be used)
2 cups heavy cream

CHOCOLATE MOUSSE

Ingredients

6 eggs, separated
5 oz semisweet chocolate
2 Tbsp butter
1 Tbsp sugar
1 tsp fresh lemon juice

SERVES 6

Separate eggs and put yolks in one large bowl and whites in another.

Melt the chocolate withbutter in the top part of a double boiler over hot but not boiling water.

Whisk the egg yolks with the sugar until thick and creamy.

Slowly pour the melted chocolate into the yolks, whisking constantly.

Beat egg whites until they are stiff. Add the lemon juice and beat the whites again.

Fold the whites slowly into the chocolate mixture, blending well.

Pour into a mold and refrigerate for at least 2 hours before serving.

Mousse may be served plain, with whipped cream, or with slivers of semisweet chocolate.

LEMON MERINGUE PIE

SERVES 6-8

Line a 10-inch tart pan with puff pastry, rolled out to 1/8 inch thick. Let it rest for one hour in the refrigerator.

Bake at 375 F for about 10–12 minutes with aluminum foil on top and beans or metal pellets on top of the aluminum to keep the pie an even shape. This will partially bake the crust. When cool, paint with semi-sweet, dark chocolate to prevent a soggy crust.

Place 6–8 crushed Amaretto cookies over chocolate layer. In a sauce pan bring to boil juice, zest, butter and sugar. Dissolve corn starch with the heavy cream.

Pour the yolks and whole eggs slowly into the boiling mixture, while stirring constantly (so as not to scorch) until it returns to a boil. Pour directly into pastry crust and top off with the sponge cake.

TO MAKE MERINGUE
Boil granulated sugar and 4 oz water until the sugar reaches 240 F. Start whipping the egg whites.

Slowly add sugar while whipping at high speed until meringue is firm and cool.

Remove from beater and either pipe with a pastry bag or pallet the meringue onto the lemon mixture and bake in the pie crust for about 10 minutes or until golden brown at 375 F.

Ingredients

puff pastry (purchase frozen)
2 oz semi-sweet dark chocolate
6-8 Amaretto cookies
1 cup fresh lemon juice
zests of 3 lemons
10 oz sugar
8 oz sweet butter
1/2 oz corn starch
2 oz heavy cream
1/2 cup egg yolks
8 eggs
1 thin layer of vanilla sponge (optional)

FOR THE MERINGUE

1 cup granulated sugar cooked to 240 F
4 oz water
1/2 cup egg whites (4-5)

NESSELRODE PIE

Ingredients

PASTRY

1 cup all-purpose flour,
   sifted
1/2 cup vegetable
   shortening
1 egg, beaten
1/2 tsp sugar
l/2 tsp salt
2–3 Tbsp cold water

SERVES 8-10

PASTRY

Thoroughly mix flour and shortening in a bowl. Blend in egg, sugar, and salt.

Slowly add water and knead the dough quickly and lightly with your fingers until it holds together.

Wrap the dough in wax paper and refrigerate for 2 or 3 hours.

Preheat oven to 450 F.

Roll out the dough flat with a floured rolling pin and fit it gently and neatly into an 11-inch pie plate.

Prick the dough with a fork, and bake for 10 or 12 minutes until the crust is lightly browned.

Set the crust aside to cool.

Prepare filling.

FILLING

Soak gelatin leaves in cold water until soft. When leaves are soft, squeeze out the water and place leaves in a small saucepan.

Melt the leaves with the 1 Tbsp rum over low heat.

Cook the 5 Tbsp sugar in the 4 Tbsp cold water until temperature reaches 225 F (test with a candy thermometer).

Put yolks, whole egg, and the 1/8 cup sugar in a large bowl and beat until fluffy.

Add cooked sugar to the eggs and beat slowly until the mixture is cool. Stir in Nesselrode fruit mix, melted gelatin, and the 2 Tbsp rum.

Whip 1 pt of the heavy cream until soft peaks form. Gently fold the whipped cream into the other ingredients.

Pour the filling into the pie shell and refrigerate for 2 or 3 hours. Whip the remaining pt of heavy cream until soft peaks form, and swirl on top of the pie.

Sprinkle with grated chocolate before serving.

Ingredients (cont'd)

FILLING
4 gelatin leaves (equal to 1 Tbsp or 1/4 oz gelatin granules)
1 Tbsp rum
5 Tbsp sugar
4 Tbsp cold water
3 egg yolks
1 egg
1/8 cup sugar
10 oz special Nesselrode fruit mix
2 Tbsp rum
1 qt heavy cream, whipped
2 oz sweet chocolate, grated

ORANGE LIQUEUR CREAM PIE

Ingredients

4 gelatin leaves (equal to 1 Tbsp or1/4oz gelatin granules)
1 Tbsp brandy
4 eggs
1/4 cup sugar
1 cup fresh orange juice
1/4 cup Cointreau
1 qt heavy cream, whipped
orange slices

SERVES 10

Soak gelatin leaves in cold water until soft.

When leaves are soft, squeeze out the water and place leaves in a small saucepan.

Melt the leaves with brandy over lowest possible heat.

Beat eggs and sugar in a large bowl until fluffy.

Thoroughly blend orange juice, Cointreau, and melted gelatin into the eggs.

Whip the heavy cream until soft peaks form.

Gently fold whipped cream into other ingredients and blend well.

Pour mixture into a mold approximately 10 inches in diameter and 2 1/2 in deep.

Refrigerate for at least 10 hours.

Unmold before serving and decorate with orange slices.

RASPBERRY OR STRAWBERRY MERINGUE PIE

SERVES 8

PASTRY
Follow the recipe for Nesselrode Pie pastry
(see p. 340).

Preheat oven to 375 F.

Beat egg whites until stiff, while gradually adding
sugar and cornstarch a little at a time.

Gently fold raspberries into 2/3 of the egg whites and
pour into the pre-baked pie shell.

Top with remaining 1/3 of the egg whites.

Sprinkle with confectioners' sugar.

Bake for approximately 15 minutes or until the pie is
golden brown.

Set aside to cool before serving.

Ingredients

FILLNG

9 egg whites
2 1/4 cups sugar
1 Tbsp cornstarch
1/4 lb fresh raspberries,
    fresh strawberries, or
    other seasonal berries
    (frozen may be used
    instead if necessary)
confectioners' sugar

RASPBERRY SOUR CREAM AND YOGURT TORTE

Ingredients

3 egg yolks
5 oz granulated sugar
5 leaves of gelatin, soaked
  until soft
8 oz plain yogurt at room
  temperature
3 oz sour cream at room
  temperature
1 cup heavy cream,
  whipped
1 10 inch vanilla sponge
  cake cut into 3 layers
simple syrup (10 oz
  boiling water, 10 oz
  sugar)
3 pt fresh raspberries
sweetened whipped cream
6 oz toasted, sliced
  almonds

SERVES 6

Warm eggs and sugar in a double boiler, being careful not to scramble the yolks. Whip on high speed in mixer bowl.

Melt drained gelatin sheets in same double boiler.

When the yolks are cold and tripled in volume, add to melted gelatin, mixing quickly to avoid lumping. Add yogurt, sour cream, and whipped cream. Blend smooth.

In a 10-in cake pan, place 1 layer of the sponge cake, lightly soaking with the simple syrup.

Pour in one-third of the sour cream/yogurt mixture. Add 1/4 of the fresh raspberries.

Spread fruit and the rest of the mixture evenly across the sponge cake, and place another layer of sponge cake on top. Repeat the above process. Refrigerate 3–4 hours.

Dip in hot water and unmold onto 10-in cardboard cake circle.

Spread sweetened whipped cream over and around the cake evenly. Sprinkle with toasted almonds.

Pipe rosettes on each portion, with raspberries and garnish.

RICE PUDDING

SERVES 6

Preheat oven to 325 F.

Toss first 9 ingredients lightly but well with the cooked rice. Be sure the mixture is blended well.

Grease a baking dish or casserole with the 2 Tbsp butter and sprinkle the bottom with 1/4 cup of the cookie crumbs.

Put rice in the dish and top with the remaining crumbs. Bake the pudding for about 50 minutes until set.

Serve hot or chilled.

Ingredients

1 1/2 cups half-and-half
pinch of salt
1/2 cup brown sugar
1/2 tsp cinnamon
1 Tbsp melted butter
1 tsp vanilla
3 eggs, beaten well
1 tsp fresh lemon juice
1/2 cup seedless raisins
2 cups cooked white rice
2 Tbsp (1/4 stick) soft
    sweet butter
1/2 cup cookie crumbs

LEMON SHERBET

Ingredients

2 cups sugar
2 cups water
pinch of salt
2 egg whites
1 cup fresh lemon juice

SERVES 6

Boil sugar, water, and salt in a small heavy saucepan for 5 minutes. Beat egg whites until they are stiff.

Pour sugar water over egg whites in a thin stream, beating constantly.

Stir in lemon juice and blend well.

Pour the mixture into a container and place in freezer until partially frozen and mushy, about 1 hour.

Beat the sherbet until smooth but not melted.

Return to the freezer until firm enough to serve.

CHOCOLATE TRUFFLE CAKE

SERVES 6

SPONGE

Preheat oven to 350 F.

Thoroughly blend almond paste with eggs and egg yolks until smooth. Add sugar and beat until mixture is stiff. Combine flour, cornstarch, and cocoa, and thoroughly mix.

Pour into a lightly greased tin 10 inches in diameter and 1/2 inch deep. Bake for approximately 45 minutes. Set aside and let cool.

FILLING

Combine the instant coffee with Cointreau. Mix the yolks with the coffee and Cointreau. Pour in melted chocolate (temperature should be 100–110 F; test with a candy thermometer), mix well.

Whip cream until soft peaks form. Very carefully fold the whipped cream into the chocolate mixture.

Cut the sponge into 4 even layers. Sprinkle Cointreau on each layer. Spread chocolate truffle filling on each layer and put one layer of sponge on top of another.

Refrigerate 3 hours. Spread sweetened whipped cream evenly over top and sides. Sprinkle shavings whipped cream.

Ingredients

SPONGE

2 oz almond paste
6 eggs
6 egg yolks
1/4 cups sugar
3/4 cup flour
3 Tbsp cornstarch
1/4 cup cocoa

FILLING

4 Tbsp instant coffee
2 Tbsp Cointreau
3 egg yolks
8 oz sweet chocolate, melted
4 cups heavy cream
Cointreau for sprinkling

2 cups sweetened whipped cream
chocolate shavings

SINFUL ANGEL CHOCOLATE MOUSSE CAKE

Ingredients
SERVES 6-8

CHOCOLATE SPONGE

8 extra large eggs
1 1/4 cups granulated
    sugar
1 3/4 cups all-purpose
    flour
4 Tbsp cocoa powder
1/2 Tbsp butter

FOR THE GANACHE
3 cups heavy cream
6 oz semi-sweet chocolate

TO MAKE THE CHOCOLATE SPONGE
In a mixing bowl, combine the eggs and the granulated sugar. Beat slightly, keeping the mixture at body temperature by putting the mixing bowl over a larger bowl containing hot water.

Sift the all-purpose flour together with the cocoa powder.

When eggs and sugar are warmed, place in a mixing machine bowl, and using the wire whip attachment, mix on high speed (5-7 minutes) until they are very light. Then reduce to medium for 4–5 minutes.

Remove the bowl from the machine and gently fold in cocoa powder and flour until just incorporated.

Pour into a buttered, 10-in floured pan and bake at 350 F for 35-40 minuites or when sponge begins to recede from the edges of the pan.

Remove and turn onto a cooling rack. When the chocolate sponge is at room temperature, wrap with plastic wrap and chill overnight.

TO MAKE THE GANACHE

Boil the cream, adding semi-sweet chocolates until melted completely. Reserve and keep warm in a double boiler.

TO MAKE WHITE CHOCOLATE MOUSSE

Whip yolks and 1 oz of sugar until it triples in volume. Add to melted chocolate with 1/2 of the whipped cream. Beat egg whites with the remaining sugar into a meringue. Fold into the chocolate mousse with half of the whipped cream (reserve half) and cookies.

TO MAKE DARK CHOCOLATE MOUSSE

Same as for white chocolate mousse, only use dark chocolate, and instead of Amaretto cookies, Amaretto liqueur. The whipped cream is the remaining half from the white mousse preparation.

Whip yolks and 1 oz of sugar until it triples in volume. Add to melted chocolate with the remaining 1 oz of sugar going into a meringue. Fold into the chocolate mousse with the other half of the whipped cream and Amaretto cookies.

In a 10-inch cake pan, place first layer on bottom and soak with cooled simple syrup. Add the mousse and spread evenly. Place the second layer of sponge over the mousse and repeat the process with the dark mousse.

Refrigerate overnight. Dip in hot water to unmold, and place on a 10-inch cake circle and pour melted ganache over the top, spreading evenly on all sides. Before glaze sets, sprinkle white and dark chocolate shavings over the top and sides of the cake.

Ingredients (con't)

WHITE CHOCOLATE MOUSSE

- 3 eggs, separated
- 2 oz granulated sugar
- 12 oz melted white chocolate
- 6 Amaretto cookies broken into small pieces
- 1 1/2 cups heavy cream

DARK CHOCOLATE MOUSSE

- 3 eggs, separated
- 2 oz granulated sugar
- 12 oz melted dark chocolate
- 3 Tbsp Amaretto liqueur

SIMPLE SYRUP

- 6 Tbsp sugar melted in 3/4 cup boiling water

FRESH STRAWBERRY SHORTCAKE

Ingredients

ROULADE (SPONGE)

3/4 cup sugar
6 eggs, separated
1 tsp lemon extract
3/4 cup all-purpose flour, sifted

FILLING

1 1/2 qt heavy cream
7/8 cup sugar
1 1/2–2 pt large fresh strawberries

SERVES 8 OR MORE

ROULADE (SPONGE)

Preheat oven to 375 F.

Separate the egss. Put yolks in one bowl and whites in another.

Beat half the sugar, egg yolks, and lemon extract for 15 minutes or until thick.

Then beat egg whites with the remaining half sugart till stiff.

Add flour and mix gently but well into the eggs.

Pour mixture onto a piece of cooking parchment and spread it evenly into a 13-inch square.

Bake approximately 15 minutes or until golden brown. Set aside and let cool.

FILLING

Whip the cream with sugar until soft peaks form. Cut the sponge in half (2 layers).

Place the bottom half of the sponge on a serving dish and cover with about 1 inch of whipped cream and a

TOASTED COCONUT LIQUEUR CREAM PIE

SERVES 10

Soak gelatin leaves in cold water until soft.

When leaves are soft, squeeze out the water and place leaves in a small saucepan.

Melt the leaves over the lowest possible heat.

Beat eggs and sugar in a large bowl until fluffy.

Thoroughly blend coconut flakes, Amaretto, and melted gelatin into the eggs.

Reserve some of the coconut to sprinkle on top of the pie.

Whip the heavy cream until soft peaks form.

Gently fold whipped cream into other ingredients and blend well.

Pour mixture into a mold approximately 10 inches in diameter and 2 1/2 inches deep.

Unmold before serving and sprinkle with coconut.

Ingredients

4 gelatin leaves (equal to 1 Tbsp or 1/4 ounce gelatin granules)
4 eggs
1/2 cup sugar
1 cup toasted coconut flakes
1/2 cup Amaretto liqueur
1 qt heavy cream, whipped

HOT FUDGE SUNDAE TOPPING

Ingredients

2 oz unsweetened
   chocolate
1 Tbsp sweet butter
1/3 cup boiling water
1 cup sugar
2 Tbsp corn syrup
1 tsp vanilla
1 tsp dark rum (optional)

ABOUT 1 CUP

Melt chocolate and butter in the top part of a double boiler over hot but not boiling water.

Stir in 1/3 cup boiling water.

Add sugar and corn syrup and blend well.

Remove sauce to direct heat.

Let the mixture boil gently, without stirring, for about 3 minutes.

Mix in vanilla and rum (optional) just before pouring over ice cream.

PRALINE NUT SAUCE

ABOUT 1 1/4–1 1/2 CUPS

Combine all ingredients in a small heavy saucepan.

Stir mixture over medium heat until just boiling.

Remove from heat and let cool.

When making sundaes, alternate a layer of the praline sauce with a layer of vanilla ice cream in a parfait glass. Top with whipped cream.

Ingredients

2 cups dark cane syrup
l/3 cup sugar
l/3 cup boiling water
1 cup pecans, coarsely
    chopped

INDEX

Page numbers in **bold** face indicate recipe page

quiche, 172

rémoulade, 311

salad, 301

sauteéd, with julienne of leek in white wine cream sauce with truffles, 174

Scampi, with fresh linguini, olive oil and herbs, 159

Shrimp and Scallop Salad with Mushrooms, 302

wiggle, 173

SIDE DISHES, *see Breads; Vegetables*

SOUP, 48-62

Bouillabaisse, 48

chowder, clam, Manhattan, 54

chowder, clam, New England, 55

chowder, fish, 53

cioppino, 56

gumbo, 57

oyster pan roast, 62

oyster stew, individual serving, 58,125

Paella, 59

red snapper, 50

she-crab, South Carolina, 51, 94

shrimp, cream of, 52

Solianka, Russian Sturgeon Stew, 61

Waterzooi, Belgian Fish Stew, 60

STEWS, *see Soups*

VEGETABLES

avocados, baked shrimp-stuffed, 160

onion rings, french-fried, 316

Oven French Fries, 314

potatoes, boiled new with parsley butter, 319

potatoes, hashed brown, 318

potatoes, duchess, 193

tomato, broiled or baked halves, 320

tomatoes, pan-fried, 321